Absolutely!

R

It was a
pleasure meeting you
both — Come back and
see us! Best of luck
Billy
May 18, 2013

ALSO BY MICAH HANKS

Magic, Mysticism and the Molecule

The UFO Singularity

REYNOLDS MANSION

AN INVITATION TO THE PAST

THE HISTORY AND STRANGE HAPPENINGS AT A
SOUTHERN ANTEBELLUM HOME

MICAH HANKS

For Evie, whose smile always keeps us guessing.

Acknowledgements

THE AUTHOR WOULD LIKE TO EXPRESS SINCERE AND HEARTFELT thanks to the following individuals, without whom this book would never have been possible: Marti Marfia for her persistent idea that a book be written about Reynolds Mansion, and most of all, her friendship, which is so very dear to me; Chris Heyes and Matthew Oakley for their help not only with the studies and experiments featured in this book, but a host of other endeavors and adventures we undertake together; Susan Davidson for providing wisdom, insight, the occasional poem, and arranging a visit with a group of real scientists who study psychic phenomenon; Lisa Northrup for being too incredible for words, and for always being there for me with her wisdom and sweet smile, even if it involves a late night séance; and finally, Billy Sanders and Michael Griffith, the owners of Reynolds Mansion, who always greet me with open arms and happy enthusiasm during my visits to their wonderful antebellum home. With any luck, this present undertaking will reflect well on each of these amazing individuals I've mentioned here, without whom life simply might not be very exciting. My thanks and blessings go out to you all.

Foreword

I REMEMBER VERY DISTINCTLY THOSE HOT SUMMER DAYS AS A child growing up in Florida, riding the bus home from school, and being let off blocks away from my house. I had to run as fast as I could on those afternoons, so I could plop down in front of the television in time to watch the weekly episode of an afternoon soap called *Dark Shadows*. The show intrigued me almost to the point of intoxication, and set into motion a lifelong love I've had for vampires, werewolves, witches, and ghosts. I was ten years old when I first heard those famous opening lines of the first episode of *Dark Shadows*, where the voice of governess Victoria Winters could be heard prefacing the beginning of her journey. What I did not know at the time, however, was that those first spoken lines would forever parallel the rest of my life just as well.

"My name is Victoria Winters. My journey is just beginning. A journey that I hope will open the doors of life to me, and link my past with my future... A journey that will bring me to a strange and dark place, to the edge of the sea, high atop Widows' Hill, to a house called Collinwood... A world I've never known, with people I've never met. People who are still only shadows in my mind, but who will soon fill the days and nights of my tomorrows..."

I have known since my early twenties that I would one day be an innkeeper. I remember traveling with a group of five friends to Savannah, Georgia and getting the opportunity to stay in a bed and breakfast owned by an elderly gentleman, whom I repeatedly reminded during my stay that I too would someday be an innkeeper. I'm not sure he believed me entirely, but on the last day of our visit, while sitting at the breakfast table, he approached me, and told me to pick any one item out of the house that I liked; then, later on when I had a bed and breakfast, I could have that item to keep someplace in my inn. I was very surprised by his generosity, but accepted nonetheless, and eventually chose a small silver tea container, which I found on the mantle in the dining room. I'm not really sure what drew me to it specifically, other than the fact that I thought it looked *really* old. Today, just as the elderly man predicted, that silver tea container sits on my dining room mantle here at Reynolds Mansion.

I often think about that unique little gift—given to me so many years ago—and for a number of reasons. First, it's because I'm not sure that the owner of that inn really believed me and my youthful aspirations of becoming an innkeeper myself; I also doubt he had any idea that one day I would look back on the gift as often as I do, and remember his generosity and how he touched my life. I'm not sure what became of him or his bed and breakfast, but I do know he was one of those many strangers we meet in life that forever change our paths. Second, that tea container reminds me of those five friends of mine with me during that visit, who never had the same opportunity to live out their dreams as I have had the great blessing of doing. My good friend Tennille, for instance, died of ovarian cancer in her mid-thirties, and another who joined us, a man named Jerry, took his own life in an accidental overdose of prescription medicine. The remaining three made various life decisions that would affect them differently throughout the years, and often leading to rather unhappy situations. Thus, I tell all my guests now who visit Reynolds Mansion that if you have a dream, no matter what your age or situation, you should make sure to take the opportunity and do what will make you happy.

The first time I saw Reynolds Mansion I knew immediately that it would be where we would live. Through all the overgrown Boston ivy, rotted porches, and overgrown gardens, something about the place still echoed in mind, "choose me, I'm the one you want!" It was very much like that two seconds that Malcolm Gladwell speaks of in his book *Blink*; I knew without a shadow of doubt that this one—this old building—definitely had something the others like it did not.

And yet, upon my arrival the words *Dark Shadows* had not merely been the title of a famous soap opera for me, but also the words that best described Reynolds Mansion before the restoration we undertook. It appeared forlorn and desolate when we first visited; it was almost *strangely* eerie, and of course, very "haunted" looking. But as the overgrown trees and ivy began to be removed, light filled the rooms and halls of the great house, and those dark shadows finally began to release all their years of history and hidden treasures.

Neither my partner Mike or I had any knowledge of Reynolds Mansion's history when we purchased the enormous estate, nor of its famous family, the enigmatic Senator from Buncombe county, his wife Evalyn Washington Mclean, the ties to the cursed Hope Diamond, or of Mamie Spears Reynolds, known to Asheville as "the child who played with the Hope Diamond." All of these hidden "shadows" over time would reach out of the past and make themselves known to us. With time, it became our goal that Reynolds Mansion should be returned in physical appearance to those times during which it had been at its prime; when the building and its inhabitants were at the height of their wealth. We were eager to bring the place back to how she might have looked in the 1930's, and in trying to achieve that, it would take years of searching and collecting history and endless conversations with people who had pieces of a vast puzzle, which we knew somehow had to be put back into place. In a sense, and despite all the information we have gathered about the home and those who have lived here over the decades, our work is only just beginning, and will continue through our tenure here, while we serve as the stewards of Reynolds Mansion.

Although my life dream was to become an innkeeper, this was not the only job that God, in his infinite wisdom, had kept in his plans for me. What came to the forefront, and of greater importance than the job of an innkeeper alone, was that both Mike and I would become caretakers of a historical property, with a history so rich and amazing that it would surpass anything either of us might ever achieve again in our lifetimes. We were destined, in a sense, to become the voice of Reynolds Mansion, and its trials and tribulations. The work of its past inhabitants would become our legacy, and we would carry their stories forward into the future.

Ultimately, the history of this place will be what we are remembered for; it will be our epitaph.

And this book that you are about to read is a part of that history. You will share in its intrigue, along with brief glimpses into not only the lives of the Reynolds family, but also where Mike and I came from, and the family members past and present that have placed our feet firmly on this path we now walk. What a tribute to those people, that we can carry forward not only with our own dreams, but with their dreams and hopes as well; their stories and lives will remain real and alive also, as we share their histories with the world. We will only be caretakers of this magnificent property for a short time, in the grand scheme of things, but it is our hope nonetheless that people from all walks of life, and all parts of the world, can continue to visit Reynolds Mansion, and perhaps for a brief moment, step back in time with us and appreciate what this building still holds of from its illustrious past.

And now, looking back as I remember the days I watched Dark Shadows and heard Victoria Winters first utter those haunting words, I now hear them as if they were written just for me: "*My name is Billy Sanders. My journey is just beginning. A journey that I hope will open the doors of life to me, and link my past with my future... A journey that will bring me to a strange and dark place, high atop a ridge on Reynolds Mountain, to a place called Reynolds Mansion... A world I've never known, with people I've never met. People who are still only shadows in my mind, but who will soon fill the days and nights of my tomorrows...*"

Billy H. Sanders
Innkeeper, The Reynolds Mansion
August 30, 2012

What man art thou that thus hast wandered here,
And found this lonely chamber where I dwell?
Beware, beware! for I have many a spell;
If greed of power and gold have led thee on,
Not lightly shall this untold wealth be won.
But if thou com'st here knowing of my tale,
In hope to bear away my body fair,
Stout must thine heart be, nor shall that avail
If thou a wicked soul in thee dost bear;
So once again I bid thee to beware,
Because no base man things like this may see,
And live thereafter long and happily.

–JAMES MARSTON, "THE EARTHLY PARADISE," 1868

A GRAND INTRODUCTION

"My name is Victoria Winters. In the short time that I've been here, Collinwood has made me a part of its strangeness... a strangeness that seems to reach out and touch everyone, and everything that lives within its walls. For the past can be a prison, not only for me, but for others; for all those driven by fears of the future."

DARK SHADOWS, EPISODE 9, AIRED 7 JULY 1966

AS A SEEKER OF THE STRANGE AND UNEXPLAINED, I'VE GROWN accustomed with time to the unusual habit of gazing at the sky, hoping to catch glimpses of things that are both incredible and otherworldly. Such anomalies may appear to us as ambiguous colored lights against the horizon, or maybe far off objects moving at sound-quaking speed. Some will even claim to have witnessed odd looking saucers that hovered over some darkened highway by night, propelled through Earth's airspace by an extraordinary mechanism that remains unparalleled by any known on Earth. Or maybe, rather than being some fantastic evidence of worlds beyond our own, these sorts of odd, unexplained illuminations one could chance to see may emanate from some place much closer to home, though still not of the physical world as we know it; *ghost lights*, perhaps.

But on the morning of June 29, 2011, there was only one glowing light that I can recall that graced the sky: passing my window, that familiar orb that accompanies every morning sunrise had begun its slow ascent, peering through a large, open iris of gleaming daylight as it crept past Reynolds Mountain in the distance.

At once, I both welcomed that daylight, and scorned the early morning that had now caught me in unrest, for it followed my first sleepless evening here in Maggie's Room. The bed to which I awoke was not my own, and though I had been welcomed into this strange and haunting place by its current residents, on this occasion my night here had not been restful. I had known, somehow, that while I had chosen to stay by myself in this cozy room on the third floor of Reynolds Mansion, I had not really been alone at all.

To be fair, I must paint myself as an exception to the general rule right from the beginning; for seldom, if ever, will you find anyone who has spent an evening at Reynolds Mansion and not claimed to have slept his or her very finest. Everything about the place, which exists today as a charming bed and breakfast on the outskirts of Asheville, North Carolina, is warm and inviting. Its comfortable rooms can never know a stranger, instead boasting familiarity and southern hospitality; the soft pillow top beds, the cozy chairs and warm baths, and even the unique, colorful décor that adorns each room's walls, welcome every newcomer into the mansion's halls and corridors invitingly, just like they were family.

To speak of family affairs, Reynolds Mansion once served as home to the very lineage that the building owes its namesake, which lasted for more than a century. Daniel Reynolds, a local farmer and hotelkeeper from nearby Bent Creek, built the home in 1847, constructing the federal style brick building on a 488-acre tract of land he purchased at a public auction. That same home Reynolds built prior to the Great War Between the States now exists among the oldest to remain standing in the area, securing its inclusion on the National Register of Historic Places. Bespeaking it's familial history, even those who enter Reynolds Mansion today will find that it still feels very much like home, especially to newcomers who book its rooms for their visits to the delightful "Paris of the South" that is Asheville, North Carolina.

Despite the warmth, history, and inviting depth of the place, Reynolds Mansion is hardly any stranger to its own brand of curiosities. Many areas throughout the house conceal discreetly placed elements of classic macabre—for instance, a reproduction of the painting featured in *The Picture of Dorian Gray* hangs on the wall adjacent to the handrail as one ascends toward the building's second floor. Passing this level of the house, one will also discover an authentic vampire hunting kit featured in the 1960 classic *The Brides of Dracula*. This odd bit of memorabilia is indeed remarkable (if not a bit startling) for its thorough inclusion of stakes, holy water, a coffin key, silver bullets, a Holy Bible, and even a hardbound copy of Montague Summers' eerie academic treatment of vampire hunting, *The Vampire, His Kith and Kin* from 1928. The entire deathly dossier rests beside a large display cabinet, whose glass casing conceals movie monsters of the silver screen, immortalized as plastic figurines striking memorable poses that have haunted many a teenage moviegoer for decades.

But perhaps most telling among all the mansion's curiosities is a masterfully gloomy portrait of Barnabas Collins—the famous bloodsucking antihero of Collinwood portrayed by Jonathan Frid in the television series *Dark Shadows*. The painting rests high above a large bookshelf, on a wall adjacent to the primary entryway as one enters the mansion's library. Beside this artistic likeness of the ancient and eerie keeper of Collinwood, the frame is adorned with a familiar looking cane; in fact, it is identical to that which Barnabas Collins owned, right down to the lunging wolf engraved into its silver handle.

It seems fitting that these curious and haunting elements would contribute to the home's décor, since like most buildings of impressive age and antiquity, Reynolds Mansion is not without its own ghosts, and in the most authentic sense. Indeed, my first sleepless night spent at the place helped affirm this as a fact in my mind, though since that time, Reynolds Mansion has become a sort of refuge for me—the proverbial home away from home, as it were—where as an author I can allow my mind's ramblings to gather, drawing together from lucid and disparate thoughts into the fitted prose expected of the printed page. So far as any writer may hope to endeavor, a place like this may only seldom—if *ever*—happen to come along, let alone the kind of inspiration and fertility it can spark in the mind. But even with its many blessings, this place and its curious mysteries will also begin to pry at one's subconscious once he stays here long enough, drawing the wandering mind into an intricate history that is equally decorated with wealth and intrigue, hope and prosperity, life and death, and of course, *longing*.

Never in my experience had I entered a place that could literally offer a window through time such as this, nor had I ever sensed such an urgency to unravel the secrets of a place and its colorful patrons so singularly. In a place like this, the past may indeed become a prison, and it became clear to me early on that

Reynolds Mansion and its ghosts are as desperate in their longing to have their odd story told as any dialogue or drama could ever hope to offer.

The sort of longing that haunts this place is the variety that can only be felt as one moves about; it echoes through the hallways and corridors, and touches one's soul as they feel its ancient vibrations. It is a longing that haunts not only those who are driven by a yearning for the past, but as the innocent young Victoria Winters said of her arrival at Collinwood, by all those driven by fears of the future, as well.

❖   ❖   ❖

As we go through life, from time to time there are certain people we meet along the road of providence that stand out among the rest. Such had been the case with the circumstances involving my introduction to Reynolds Mansion; it began with a phone call I received late in the morning, and quite unexpectedly, on a cool day in May 2011. I was delighted when I answered to find it was an old friend on the line, long missed, but hardly forgotten.

"Micah, this is Marti Marfia. Gosh, it's been so long… how are you?"

Marti's voice sounded cheerful and upbeat, as it had always been. It seemed like we hadn't spoken in ages; but at that choice moment, I can't truly claim that I hadn't expected to hear from her. In fact, Marti had been on my mind just one day earlier, and now— as if on cue—she had apparently decided to call right out of the blue. Then again, Marti had always displayed a curious penchant for this particular brand of mind reading over the years, and I could number many occasions where she had exhibited an apparent sense for knowing things she couldn't possibly have been made privy to already. Though a bit more seldom, there were also times that she even seemed to know things before they happened.

"Marti, it's so funny you would call," I admitted. "You had literally been on my mind just yesterday." For other kinds of folks, this might have seemed only strange and serendipitous. For Marti and I, it was far more than mere chance that she had been on my mind, and once we had time to catch up a bit regarding the goings on of our families, work, and life in general, the conversation came around to our apparent reason for the occasion.

"Well listen, part of my wanting to call you today has to do with this bed and breakfast I'm working for now. The place is just so incredible, and Micah, I'm telling you, it has so many *ghosts*... I've just never seen anyplace quite like it."

"Ghosts?" I asked, chuckling a bit.

"No really," Marti assured me. "This place is unlike any I've ever been. The rooms, the history, it's just... it's strange. The only way I could describe it would be to say that from the moment I first arrived, I have felt the strongest sensation that I've been here before..." Her voice trailed off for a moment before she caught herself. "Micah, you wouldn't have any time today to..."

"Goodness Marti, I'd love to," I interrupted. "I just have so much on my schedule. Deadlines being neglected, including one of these essays that's going in that new anthology for the publishers up in New York. Then I'm also heading out of town at around four o'clock this afternoon."

"Oh, I understand," Marti replied. We continued to chat, but I could tell her persistence was merely lying dormant. Marti has a way of courting a subject, and when she's ready to sell you on an idea, just *watch out*. Another few minutes passed as she continued describing her fascination with the place before she tried again.

"You know, I wish you had even just a couple of hours today," she began. Had she known that I was already accepting the futility of warding off her argument, I might have stopped her; but as she continued telling me about this odd place, a very old mansion on a lonely hill past the North end of town, neither her appeals to me for an impromptu visit, nor the apparent allure of the place itself, could be resisted with ease.

"Well what can I say, Marti?" I laughed.

"How about saying yes?" she advised. There was a brief pause.

"I suppose I could clear out just a few hours," I said, relenting. I've since learned not to engage Marti Marfia head-on in a battle of charms—knowing full well that she'll win—unless I'm fully prepared to modify my schedule for the rest of the day. For the time being, providence had yet again led me away from my desk, and before I knew it, I was grabbing my coat and trudging off on another unplanned adventure into the heart of the past, or for all I knew, something else.

I did know, however, that I'd be in good company.

❖   ❖   ❖

As a prelude to our afternoon together, Marti invited me to her home in Weaverville first for coffee. Billy Sanders, the present owner of Reynolds Mansion, had been in town running errands, and needed a little time to wrap things up before we arrived. He told Marti he would be back by one, however, and after we finished our coffee, we hopped in our cars and caravanned back toward Reynolds Mountain.

Arriving and seeing the grounds for the first time was the first of many timeless experiences at the Mansion. We parked in a gravel lot designated for visitors behind the building, and as Marti led me through the garden toward the back door, the beauty of the flora took me immediately. Vibrant red and yellow droplets of color swirled in miniature seas of green, and stems danced to the breeze as if keeping beat with our footsteps. The carefully laid brick pathway meandered between these swaying patches of color, and as we made our way along, I nearly had to remind myself to take this opportunity to look at the house itself.

The antebellum brick home standing before me certainly had a majesty all to itself; three floors stacked onto one another, housed within a beautiful red brick outer structure, faced westward, while a smaller wing extending to the north followed the natural ridgeline, housing the kitchen area. A single large chimney rose from this smaller portion of the house, while a similar pair could be seen emerging from the rooftop above the main building. Beautiful, elaborate porches also canvassed the building's lower levels along the south side, with light blue ceilings and white Tuscan columns that carried the modillion along continuous lintels in the style of the Colonial Revival. And yet, as breathtaking as the building itself had been, the rear garden and its décor had proven already to be an incomparable show-stealer.

"Mr. Sanders must have quite a groundskeeper," I said, still in awe of the entire place and its beauty.

"Oh no, that's all Billy's handiwork," Marti said. "He and Michael are the only ones here, and Billy does all the yard work himself."

"Incredible," I added. "Certainly has a green thumb, doesn't he?"

We continued along, and approaching the entrance, another small batch of plants captured my eye to the left of the door, situated inside a small terrarium.

"Marti look, these are pitcher plants," I said, delighted. "And flytraps, and even a sundew. I used to love growing carnivorous plants when I was a child." In particular, I can remember my father and mother bringing me a small potted Venus Flytrap when I was just a boy, and marveling at how the insides of the little green pedals would darken and turn red, springing open like begging mouths as the plant grew, consuming the occasional fly or other insect for extra nutrients.

"Well just wait until you come inside," Marti assured me. There was an undertone of irony to this statement, and to the circumstances in general. I remember finding it slightly odd that, despite the fact that she worked here, Marti had been sure to ring the doorbell this first time she brought me; this evoked a sense that we were both about to become initiates into whatever strange magic may await us within.

Only a few moments passed before Billy Sanders appeared in the doorway, greeting us. He was tall, dark skinned, and blonde, with his hair trimmed close around the sides and spiked straight up in the front. Accompanying him were too adorable British bulldogs, grunting excitedly as he opened the door. Billy greeted Marti with a hug, and quickly extended a hand toward me.

"Hi Micah, welcome to Reynolds Mansion." The easy, southern tones underlying his accent reminded me of the Sunshine State, and of friends I knew, originally from Florida. Despite his clean-cut appearance, the only facet that betrayed his daily schedule—and the kind of work it entailed—was the slight roughness of his hand as it grasped mine.

"Glad to meet you," I said, gesturing toward the garden. "Marti and I were just admiring your work out here." A slight grin found its way toward the corner of his mouth, as he thanked us and brought us in.

Scarlett (left) and Rhett. Photo by Shary Connella

"By the way, this is Scarlett, and Rhett," Billy said as his bulldogs waddled along beside him. Rhett's under bite and the lines of his drooping jowls almost gave the impression that he had a thin moustache running parallel to his lips, which trembled as he barked with excitement. Scarlett, much like her namesake, was more petite, and there was even a mild redness to her eyes, causing her to have what looked at times like a concerned expression. Both were fitted with stout little bodies that wiggled as they barreled along, and a tiny nub of a tail that protruded from each one's rump.

Upon entering, I found the interior of the house surprisingly cool, despite the heat that had begun to pick up as the day wore on. The air inside, rather than hot and stale like most buildings of its age, was cool and perfumed with a light scent that smelled like oranges, which Billy had procured and managed to have dispersed throughout the mansion's three levels. Almost immediately, we were taken into the dining room adjacent to the main entryway.

My private tour of Reynolds Mansion had begun.

I was first shown a large, romantic painting of a dark-haired Cajun girl, hanging on the wall above the master fireplace in the dining room. Her dress was long and light, contrasting sharply with the dark branches of the cypress trees that swirled in and around from behind her.

"Micah, be sure and watch her eyes as you move around the room," Marti advised. "You'll see how they look like they're following you as you go."

Indeed, the Cajun beauty's eyes, resting darkly on her light, playful expression, would seem to glide along and follow me virtually anywhere I chose to stand. Billy explained that the painting, originally from the Chretien Plantation in Louisiana, had only one other owner before him; in truth, the very fact that he obtained it at all had been serendipitous.

"Michael had gone and asked about this painting for me, and the folks selling it were asking $2,800 dollars for it. They even had a sign warning that if you tried to get them to lower their price, they'd triple what they were asking! Well, I loved the painting, and told Michael I was going back down there to see what I could do, regardless. So I walked in, and I asked about it, and the old gentleman who was selling it offered me the same price again that Michael had been told. I just couldn't afford it, and I told him that.

"Well at that point, I had decided there wasn't anything more I could do. I was turning to leave, but then he stopped me. He said, 'young man, you like this painting, don't you?' I told him I did—that I loved it. I had hoped maybe he would bring his price down a little, but I never expected what he was about to say: 'My wife would probably kill me, but I'll let you have it for seven hundred.' I couldn't believe it, but I paid him right then, and brought it home!"

Billy also told us that he had inquired about having the painting professionally cleaned, but that for a piece of art of its age and delicacy, he would be forced to part with it for up to three years in order to complete the entire process; hence, the painting has remained in its present state, and with its current owner ever since he acquired it. However, I was already entertaining the idea that perhaps there could be more to the painting's allure than just the story associated with it, or even the wandering eyes of Felicity, it's lovely Cajun subject.

"I've had a lot of problems with it," Billy admitted, "especially when I've moved places where I brought it along. In one place we lived, I had just mounted it there on the wall, and that night when I came into the kitchen, every one of the cabinet doors in the kitchen was standing wide open. Well, I figured Michael or somebody had been in there, so I just went through and closed each cabinet.

"The next morning, Michael had gone into the kitchen and described the same thing. He came in and asked me if I had opened all the cabinets, and whether I left them that way for some reason!" Billy told us that this same series of events had taken place each time he had moved to a new residence, but only when that particular painting had been with him. Here at Reynolds, however, he admitted it had been hard to tell how much of the unusual activity might have been associated with the painting, and how much might have been indigenous to the home and its unusual history.

It was obvious as we continued our tour of Reynolds Mansion that Billy had more than merely happened across odd bits of information about his new home. If anything, his ability to recall detailed history about the mansion, its former residents, and the belongings in it, betrayed his deep passion for knowing all he could about the place. He spoke of the slaves that worked to build the place—all fifteen of them—as if he had known each one. He could describe the harvesting of clay from nearby Beaver Lake, used in the formation of the bricks that made up this building's massive structure, as though he had watched the entire process while it was underway. As was quite apparent by now, Billy had worked very hard at uncovering every tidbit he could about the building's unique history, and I found it incredible the way he managed to recall specific names, dates, and places, as though he had actually known each person or location he mentioned. In a sense, he was a man born not of his own time, and Billy Sanders spoke of Reynolds Mansion with the passion of someone who had been here throughout all it's times and trials. He knew it well, and none of its secrets seemed to elude him.

As we entered the library, I was amused upon first noticing the paintings of Barnabas Collins and Collinwood's dark denizens that adorned the walls. However, Billy quickly directed my attention to something far more magnificent: a beautiful blue diamond, encased in silver, displayed within a small glass fixture by the window. One would hardly need to be a jeweler—or even a jewel collector—to find it breathtaking; like some ancient stone a faithful heiress would wear, gifted by her betrothed, disguising a secret magical cornerstone to some vast and curious faerie tale... why then, in all its magnificence, did it look *familiar*?

"This is a replica of the stone featured in the film *Titanic*, which had been based on the Hope Diamond," Billy explained. "Senator Bob Reynolds' wife, Evalyn Washington MacLean, had inherited the diamond from her mother, who kept it in the family, and she wore it while she lived here with the Senator."

I stared into the glimmering hollows of the stone's vast depth, and it became easy to imagine it as being more than a mere replica. A gorgeous deep azure radiated up through the glass at me as I peered over it, the facets of its girdle and pavilion rounding out like a nutshell, sparkling and hardened by passing eons. The real Hope Diamond, believed to be more than one billion years old and with an estimated worth of $250 million, now resides with the trusted caretakers at the Smithsonian in Washington, where it receives more visits from connoisseurs and collectors worldwide than any other piece of art, sparing only da Vinci's Mona Lisa. As I observed the unique replica before me, Billy continued with stories of how Evalyn had once used to hang it around the family dog's neck at their Washington home, letting him run around in the yard while wearing the priceless stone; an incredible prospect, indeed, if not a slightly terrifying one. But perhaps even more frightening had been the notion that this peculiar stone had also harbored a dark side: even today, the Hope Diamond is still famous for its "curse," which was said to have haunted many of its owners throughout their lifetime. For some, its mythic allure and unsettling air had been much worse, and was even credited with claiming the lives of those who had worn it.

Before leaving the library, Billy shared with me a few of the books in his collection that ranked among his favorites, before he, Marti and I began our ascent toward the upper floors of the building. The third floor, as it was explained to me, had been the place where all the spooks had apparently chosen to reside, with stories of odd happenings on this level of the building dating back at least to the 1960s, when a local broom making business had been operated out of the home's downstairs. We climbed the final staircase, ascending through a large opening that in years past had been closed off with a trap door in the winter, capturing precious heat within the first two floors, and made our way down a thin hallway. Billy paused in front of another old display cabinet here, and I noticed a lovely and curious oil painting of Argentinean First Lady Eva Perón hanging above it; another of our guide's unique and eclectic choices among artistic additions. Reaching into the cabinet, he withdrew a number of odd knickknacks, telling the stories behind each: among these were a dowsing rod, an old replica flintlock pistol, and a medicine bottle labeled "APOTHECARY ASIFIDITY" filled with a foul smelling powder. This handy substance had hailed from the days of holistic treatments that amounted to being little more than "snake oil" medicines; a variety of curative elixirs for which Asheville had once been famous.

"Now look at this hairpin," Billy said, producing the rusty remnant of jagged wire in his hand. "This was found laying on the bed in the room where people still claim they see the ghost of Annie Lee Reynolds. Keep in mind, I had just made the bed only a few hours earlier, and there was no way, to my knowledge, that it could have gotten there. There weren't even any guests staying in the room at that time." Taking the hairpin, I turned it between my fingers, looking it over closely. Had one of the Reynolds ghosts left an old possession lying in plain sight, perhaps as some sort of calling card? It was an entertaining notion, however likely the actual prospects might have been.

We continued down the hall to the final two rooms on the third floor, the entrances to each standing directly across from one another on either side of the hall. Billy didn't have quite as much to say about these two rooms, aside from the fact that they were the last two guest rooms on the final floor the house. We all but glanced in the room on the right, a cozy little suite called *Inez*, which had been decorated in tones of scarlet red. We then briefly entered the doorway across from it, which led into to a quaint little bedroom named *Vera*, with dark blue trimmings.

It was in this room that I first began to notice an odd, heavy sensation. None of the other rooms had felt quite like *this*. There was uncomfortable warmth in here, a sort of mugginess, emanating perhaps from the heat gathering on the rooftop outside. But it seemed that there was something else here too, though I was having trouble placing it. Acting almost on impulse alone, I darted through a doorway to my left, which led into a dark bathroom with no windows. The only illumination at all came from a small nightlight attached above a sink by the doorway, and then the light from it that reflected off the tub behind me…

As I turned to look, within moments, the reason for my discomfort became obvious. I was treated, in my mind's eye, to the image of an old man lying partially submerged in this antique tub; his gaunt cheeks and pale skin gave him an unsettling appearance. Wisps of his remaining white hair clung to his scalp in clumps above his ears, and I could even discern the darkened lentiginous freckles that peppered his skin, especially along the bald ridges of his head. I could imagine this all so strongly that I might have even caught the reflection of that same nightlight shimmering against his ghastly paleness, had it not been for the fact that this frightening object of my present unrest had been absent, at least in the purely physical sense. A strange vision of disquiet that had erupted into my mind—that was all—and yet the stranger's deathly visage lingered with me for several moments afterward as we left the strange room, tracing our path from earlier as we reentered the hallway. For the time being, I chose to remain silent about this strange, unsettling vision.

Finally, we came back to the top of the stairway, but rather than beginning our descent toward the lower levels of the house, Billy led us into one final room on this floor that we hadn't been shown.

"This one is called Maggie's room," he told us. "It's in here that a lot of the folks who stay here report having the most activity."

"Activity?" I asked, feigning misunderstanding. "What kind of activity do you mean, Billy?"

"This is the room where most people who have stayed here say they've had things happen. If what they say is correct, Maggie's room seems to be one of the most haunted in the entire mansion."

Among the odd happenings that occurred here were the sorts of mind games and trickery often associated with haunted places; many guests would awaken to find the small chair that stood beside the closet had been moved, inexplicably. Sometimes it

would be repositioned in such a way that whomever might sit in it would have been staring directly at the bed, or perhaps those asleep in it. One couple that had stayed in the room recently had arrived late, and rather than putting their belongings away, had hastily rested them on the top of the bed before leaving for a night in town. Upon returning a few hours later, they found the door wouldn't seem to budge, despite having been unlocked. After several unsuccessful attempts at getting into the room, the guests finally relented, and went to notify Billy, who was forced to have Michael access the room from the *outside*, climbing in through one of the exterior windows. There, upon entering, he was treated to yet another puzzling circumstance: all the guests' belongings had been piled into the floor, leveled against the base of the door! If indeed there were any ghosts here, they seemed to prefer that guest's belongings be put away, rather than being piled onto the bed.

And of course, this was the very same room where the small, rusty hairpin had manifested on the clean white blanket tops. It had been the apparent calling card, Billy surmised, for a particularly mischievous young ghost believed to be one of the home's early occupants: the original owner's youngest daughter, miss Annie Lee Reynolds.

"And when you come spend your first night here with us, Mr. Hanks," Billy said turning again towards me, "this is the room where *you* will be staying, too."

Two

NIGHTTIME VISITORS

Roger Collins: "Well did you meet any ghosts?"
Victoria Winters: "No, but I dreamed about them all night long. I must have wakened up twenty times thinking there was something in my room."

DARK SHADOWS, EPISODE 71, AIRED 3 OCTOBER 1966

IT HAD ONLY BEEN A FEW HOURS SINCE I ARRIVED AT REYNOLDS Mansion, and as the black curls of darkness began to unfold themselves throughout the house, it felt as though the space between the walls in every room had slowly begun widen, opening up vast expanses of mystery that couldn't exist in daylight.

The idea that Annie Lee Reynolds' spirit had lingered long enough in this place to become one of the building's prolific ghosts—among others purported to live here—had stemmed from a number of curious circumstances, many of which involved the appearance of a strange young girl along the grounds of Reynolds Mansion. While some of the descriptions varied, one of the more

21

consistent traits people often described of the mansion's daintiest specter had been the way she wore ribbons in her long brown hair; incidentally, a picture of Annie Lee Reynolds as a teenager, hanging by the exit to the balcony on the second floor, bore a striking resemblance to the ghost so many claimed they had seen while visiting.

Still, supposing that Annie Lee might be the apparition in question presents its own problems, since she hadn't died as a child. Born in July of 1866, Annie Lee lived to within only days of reaching her eighty-second birthday, passing away on Independence Day, 1948. Indeed, it would seem strange if Annie Lee, after living a full life, had chosen to return to the mortal realm to carry out her unfinished business as a manifestation from a much earlier period in her lifetime... that is, if we are to accept the conventional notion that a ghost is indeed a restless spirit of the deceased.

Regardless, I soon learned that one of the more vivid encounters with the lonely young lady of Reynolds had taken place only a few months prior to my own first arrival here, at which time the mansion had not yet opened for business as a bed and breakfast. On the afternoon in question, two ladies happened to stop by with interest in asking about renting the location for an upcoming baby shower. It was on the porch in front of the house, opposite of the garden where I had initially met the home's illustrious new owner, that an introduction of a very different kind had taken place... and all within moments of Billy's arrival at the door to greet the two ladies.

"Mr. Sanders," one of the women asked once they both had entered the building, "Whose daughter was it we saw standing inside before you came to the door? It seemed like nothing we could do would get her attention."

"Daughter?" Billy asked, perplexed. "Well, there aren't any families staying here right now. We've not even opened to the public yet, and I'm the only one in the building for the time being. What did she look like?"

The women described that the girl they saw had sandy brown hair, tied up in ribbons, and was wearing a long dress. As the two visitors had been waiting outside the front door, both of them saw this young woman standing on the main stairway between the parlor and the library; but after trying for several minutes to get her attention, the visitors finally decided to walk around to the other side of the building, where they were eventually greeted by Billy at the back door. It was curious indeed, the way the child had ignored them completely, and if anything, it had almost seemed as though the young girl they observed couldn't hear or see them at all.

"When we tried getting her attention, she just ignored us, like she hadn't even known we were there," one of the women complained. Again, Billy assured them that there were no others staying with him at the mansion at that time, and that he was in fact the only person present on the grounds.

"Who knows, maybe she was an unfriendly ghost."

❖　　❖　　❖

As darkness enveloped Reynolds Mansion, Billy and I sat in the library, talking about the many strange appearances this young girl had made throughout various parts of the home. Earlier in the evening, Marti had joined us as well, but had only been able to stay long enough to share a few drinks at sunset; she and Billy had enjoyed a bottle of wine, while I sipped on a sweet ginger-flavored brandy that Billy kept in the parlor across the hall from where we now sat talking.

"I know it sounds crazy, but I've wondered often whether separate instances of time couldn't run parallel to one another," Billy explained. "You know, like the past running parallel alongside our present. Maybe when we see ghosts, we're able to see into a past that exists right beside us... like another dimension."

I too had found myself pondering curious circumstances akin to what my host was describing, and was certain that such possibilities were no doubt kept fresh on the minds of those who had their brushes with any of Reynolds Mansion's lingering specters. But why was it that Annie Lee—if that's even who the spirit of the young girl being seen actually was—always seemed to shy away from direct conversation with the guests that managed to see her? Billy shared a very interesting story that hinted at a reason for this; it involved a well-known psychic named Kristy Robinett, who visited the mansion several months prior to my own introduction here. Indeed, the mansion and its curious history had managed to attract the interest of a number of film crews and television personalities in the short time it had been open for business under Billy's supervision, and on the occasion in question, a now very familiar turn of events had revealed itself while Robinett and the others had been filming for a television series that followed the exploits of a group of paranormal investigators.

At one point during her survey of the mansion, Robinett had chosen to enter Maggie's Room. There, having been given no prior information about the building, it's past occupants, or the ghosts others had professed seeing, she claimed she was able to see a young girl in the room. However, the child hadn't seemed capable of perceiving any events that had been transpiring around her, instead merely sitting alone, focused on her playthings. Robinett believed that this had been because of separate instances of time that were transpiring concurrently, perceptible only by certain individuals at particular times. In essence, when she had claimed to be able to see Annie Lee, it was as though she had peered into a sort of window through time, where young Annie Lee Reynolds sat in the room in a separate temporal state, unable to perceive events transpiring in a future long after her own passing.

Robinett hadn't been the only one to notice things in Maggie's Room that remained unseen to others nearby, however. Billy noted that even Scarlett and Rhett, as they would run along the hallway toward the top of the staircase, would occasionally stop outside Maggie's Room, staring at the bed and even wagging their tails expectantly, as though there had been someone friendly-looking inside that they were eager to play with.

"There were some other interesting things that Kristy Robinett said while she was here," Billy told me as he refilled my brandy glass. "Just to your left as you enter the back door, there is a guest room—the only one in the entire house with carpeted floors—called *Lila*. It was intended as the original master bedroom. It connects with this part of the house through a doorway, which I keep blocked off these days." Billy gestured toward a concealed door in the corner of the library as he said this.

"In that room, Kristy said she saw the spirit of a young girl. But unlike the little girl on the third floor, this one spoke to her."

"And what did she tell her?" I asked. By now, I was nearly expecting to see one of these ghosts walk in and join us for a nightcap.

"This one was really amazing," Billy said. "She told her that she had been embalmed here."

"*Embalmed?*" I exclaimed, nearly choking on the brandy that burned my throat.

"Yes, she told her that she had been embalmed here at the mansion. Now keep in mind, we never told Kristy Robinett anything about this building, and while it's possible she might have gotten some details elsewhere, we didn't have that kind of information available on our website yet, either."

"Well why in the hell would there be mention of a girl being embalmed here in the first place?" I asked.

"See, that's where it gets interesting. Even though Kristy couldn't have known any of this as far as I understand, Michael and I had learned by then that Reynolds Mansion had served as an osteopathic sanitarium for a while during the 1920s, under a woman named Elizabeth Smith. However, Nat Augustus Reynolds, the stepfather of Senator Bob, had been a funeral director here in town around the same time. When he and Mamie Reynolds moved back into the mansion in the early 1930s, the building by the pool, which was originally designed to be a garage, had been where some of the embalming practices were carried out. It all happened right here on the property."

"Wow," I said. "That's not really the kind of thing that you expect from old homes. I mean, it seems pretty normal for people to describe seeing ghosts, but when they say they've been embalmed, and a funeral director had been doing *just that* literally across the driveway, it seems to lend itself a little to the notion that your psychic friend might have been on to something."

Of course, I found it curious that, while there was this intriguing notion of "parallel time" we'd previously been toying with, Robinett had clearly seemed to communicate directly with one of the specters she encountered here, too. In other words, perhaps not *all* the ghosts people were said to have seen here at Reynolds Mansion were just events from the past, replayed before an audience of baffled observers in the present day. Furthermore, if Robinett's claims are to be believed, this ghost she met had certainly given some rather unique details about its afterlife, right down to knowledge of the embalming process its own physical body had undergone. Perhaps if unique physical circumstances could in some way exist that allowed for a more traditional notion of a "ghost" to manifest, then for all we know, there might also be conditions where people can perceive "windows" to past events, just as well.

Many believe that each person is born intended to fulfill some kind of purpose in life. Some will fully embrace whatever it is that they sense as being their *calling*, while others may only happen upon some aspect of their intended purpose by mere chance alone. In my case, it became obvious at an early age that my interest in the fringe and unusual aspects of life would lead me into pursuit of uncanny mysteries; a veritable quest for the shadows that linger past the still hours, and the hope that there might exist some rational basis for reuniting such oddities with respected science. For me, this has indeed manifested itself as a calling; but our sense of longing to fulfill certain things might not only pertain to our operations in this lifetime. Others might have us believe that when we don't fulfill our life's greater purposes, or perhaps when we are prevented from doing so by untimely death, our spirits will linger among the living in a restless state, with hope of caring for the proverbial "unfinished business" that is said to trouble many specters of the dead.

In other words, being a ghost isn't perceived as being a desirable thing, per se. And yet, the thrill and appeal often associated with "ghost hunting," popularized in the modern era by television shows that have made a hobby—or even a business—out of the practice of parapsychology, is obvious. Our culture in the West has become permeated by the notion that anyone can gather a few quirky gadgets like electromagnetic field detectors, infrared cameras, laser thermometers, and other devices, and with little or no practice, they can suit up and enter the homes of the willing, pursuing their passion for contact with realms beyond on a nightly basis.

I began as one of these researchers in the early 2000s, still wet behind the ears and eager to go into old homes, churches, and historic buildings to try and find evidence of an afterlife. I also learned rather quickly that investigations of the paranormal, contrary to what we see on television programs, seldom (if ever) involve the terror and thrill many self-proclaimed investigators and their respective research organizations claim to encounter. While I had been intrigued early on by he appearance of things such as electromagnetic anomalies in an environment purported to be haunted, my experiences trying to disseminate anything of value from these sorts of observations were sparing, at best. For instance, while many researchers will claim to observe weak electric fields that appear to move about an environment as though they were intelligently controlled, it remains an obvious fact that there is no way to prove conclusively what the source of that kind of energy may really be. Nonetheless, the paranormal investigator will often cite this kind of observation as some kind of proof of an otherworldly presence. I eventually found myself asking why, exactly, this should be the case.

One reason for my skepticism had been the obvious problem with there being no physical presence in the room—a body, in other words—to produce the energy. But why should this be an issue, if the idea that a ghost being able to manifest in the first place must involve the presence of some kind of energy just as well?

One reason for my concern in this regard involves the convolution that erupts between observing how an electromagnetic field meter behaves in two very different circumstances; namely, these would be in the presence of a human being, versus an empty room in an environment purported to be haunted. Certain quality EM detectors available for purchase, such as the TriField Natural EM Meter, allow the user to adjust variable controls on the device that tune it to react to specific kinds of natural electromagnetic fields. One setting will perceive radio and microwave sources, for instance, while another may even react to the natural magnetic field our bodies produce. But here's where things begin to get tricky: when a device such as this is capable of reacting to the human body, many paranormal investigators will use this as justification for the idea that if the device behaves in a similar way when there is no one standing nearby, then perhaps the meter is measuring some energetic presence that a spirit is able to possess, even in the *absence* of a physical body.

While this may very well be the case, the problem with this logic is that the more likely source within the human body for energy a device like this may react to would stem from the body itself. We are bioelectric beings, in the sense that our bodies, as a byproduct of being alive and expending energy, produce electric fields that are indeed measurable. Therefore, if we accept this easily provable precept, we must then ask what, if anything, in the absence of that physical body would still cause an EM meter to react in such a way? Justifying this mystery with the otherwise scientifically unquantifiable notion of there being a spirit that can exist outside the body presents a troublesome leap in logic, knowing so little as we do about the true nature of that thing we call the human soul.

Approaching this same conundrum from the opposite perspective, on many occasions I've observed investigators using lower quality, consumer grade EM meters to detect various kinds of energy fields in an environment, pointing to the inexplicable nature of the circumstances as "proof" of something, due entirely to the way their instruments seem to react to an unidentifiable source. In these circumstances, it is often the case that these devices are specifically calibrated for use in detecting electromagnetic pollution in the home or office, like excessive electromagnetic radiation stemming from microwave ovens and other household devices. However, meters that are designed for use in such applications around the home are typically not capable of measuring energies the human body produces. Thus, we must also ask what kind of energy, which the body *does not produce,* would suddenly manifest once the spirit exists alone? Furthermore, why would this mysterious source conveniently become measurable using the same devices that determine the safe distances one can operate around various electrical appliances? Does a soul or spirit only become capable of being observed and measured scientifically *after* it leaves the body? This hardly seems plausible.

Thus, the final element that would aspire to reconcile these two issues would be to assume that certain spirits of the dead are able to conjure energies from the environment around them in a unique way, allowing them to manifest as ghosts. It is this act of drawing the energies together, the paranormalist would assume, that becomes measurable using EM meters and other devices, rather than the soul itself. Following this logic, one might even assume that such energies *must* be present, since it would obviously require some energy source for an apparition to be able to manifest in the first place.

While this scenario may work well as long as we're only speculating, we cannot make such assumptions without evidence to support them, and then use these as the justification for similar varieties of unexplainable phenomena. In other words, we can't go about taking various observations out of context, and then use them to justify a preconceived notion such as the idea that an old building might be "haunted," or that ghosts are always, without question, "spirits of the dead." Furthermore, it becomes dangerous when we use bold, unproven speculation as a foundation for those observations, uniting them under the claim of being "scientific." Such is the very essence of pseudoscience, and engaging in such frivolity no more aids us in understanding our world's mysteries than following suit with the ostrich, who, as Pliny the Elder noted long ago, would rather bury her head in the sand than to perceive the real world that exists around her.

My intention here is not to sound like a debunker, nor is it to try and make the case for ghosts and related phenomena being mere fantasy. Quite the contrary, it is my feeling that ghosts are not only very real, but that belief in their existence points to a strong undercurrent within our own cultural and psychological makeup. The prolific presence of what appear to be encounters with spirits of the dead in cultures around the world also has scientific implications, in the sense that it may point to physics anomalies that could exist within the framework of our reality, suggesting that time and space are indeed not entirely what they seem to be. There are religious implications here just as well, for while some will warn that anything professing to be the ghost of a dead loved one is really some malevolent minion of the dark side, for others the presence of deceased spirits among the living is proof that some aspect of ourselves—whatever the proverbial other side may truly entail—does continue on after we die.

In learning to think critically about claims of the paranormal, my worldview began to change with time, and eventually it became clear to me that using "scientific" meters and cumbersome gadgetry when trying to observe and understand the supernatural perhaps did more harm than good. As paranormal researcher and writer Jeff Belanger wrote in the introduction to his book *The World's Most Haunted Places,* "Exploring the paranormal isn't just about great stories—though that's a part of it. And it's not science, though many have made attempts to apply science to the subject. The paranormal is about delving into big questions within all of us. It's a spiritual and philosophical quest, full of emotion, pitfalls, problems, excitement, history, psychology, and a whole range of human experiences."

To understand these human experiences better for myself, I felt that my best attempts at reconciling with the unexplained would be to simply experience them as a human. Therefore, with my coming to Reynolds mansion, it had been Marti's idea all along to have me stay here not only to learn about the place and its history, but to observe the strange presences which many claimed were somehow related to the mansion's past. Perhaps there really were the spirits of former residents here, who have come and gone over the decades; or perhaps these odd happenings only amount to being energetic diffusion bouncing between the building's walls, sometimes creating a wrinkle in space-time that allows those of us in the present day a glimpse at events from a past well before our own time. Whatever the case, my toolbox for the occasion had been Spartan in its simplicity: I brought with me to Reynolds Mansion only a quality pen and a notepad. My cell phone would keep the time when I strayed from view of any number of the antique grandfather clocks that adorned the mansion's walls, and the Cabernet swirling in the base of my glass would help maintain lucidity of the senses as I wandered throughout the darkened mansion's halls. The sparse lighting in each of the rooms I entered would inspire any hope for aptitudes I might develop in terms of spirit-sensing, and my imagination would no doubt work with diligence at fueling my curiosity, pursuing every thumping and bumping throughout the house as though it had been the literal rapping of some spectral occupant in an adjacent room.

Tonight, I aspired to make acquaintance with new friends at this elderly place; if any made their presence known to me, I could count on the fact that they too would be of a *very* old variety, and that I would greet then armed with little more than my senses.

As my host's evening had begun to resolve, I joined Billy while he continued sharing bits of history about the place during our ascent toward the third floor. Even as far back as the 1960s, there had been stories of a curious thumping that could be heard coming from the upstairs; the weird occurrences had been related during the brief tenure held here by a specialty broom company, at which time a group of "hippies" in their employ had lived downstairs. One local writer, covering the company's operation in an editorial for the area newspaper, referenced the stories about ghosts on the mansion's highest level, and wrote disdainfully of the place in it's then-present state; the building was compared vaguely with Toad Hall, in a glum nod to Kenneth Grahame's wealthy and aristocratic anuran of *The Wind in the Willows*. To the home's previous owners, one might surmise the broom makers taking residence in the downstairs at that time would have shown more than a passing resemblance to the weasels and ferrets of the Wild Wood, which eventually overtook Mr. Toad's lavish home in Grahame's great fable of the Thames valley.

Upon reaching his suite, Billy took a few moments to share some of the obscure foreign films in his rich collection of cinema with me. The unconventional style and taste opined throughout the former Reynolds family home obviously had its genesis in Billy's appreciation for classics of suspense and the macabre, and many of the same films whose characters now adorned the mansion's walls and alcoves were kept here by the owner for viewing. Following our survey of his film collection I bid my host goodnight, and heading back downstairs into the calm quiet of the shadows, I made my way to the back of the house, where I would begin my vigil for the evening.

Entering the dining room, I added a splash of fresh Cabernet to my glass, and sat down at the long dining room table on the end nearest to the kitchen. I began by marking the time at the top of a clean page in my notebook—it was 11:16 PM—and then sank back into the chair, listening carefully to the sounds the house made as the heat of day abandoned it to the cool night air outside. As I waited, listening, I would occasionally glance over my shoulder toward the doorway that led into the hall, waiting to catch a glimpse of some thin, pale face peering around the corner; maybe it would be one of the embalmed ghosts, or perhaps the young girl that had already revealed her presence to so many others who had visited here. I would occasionally note my observations, relating various things about my surroundings.

> 11:16 PM: I'm now sitting at the dining room table having a glass of wine, observing things about the environment. Aside from a few slightly ominous sounds coming from various parts of the house, all is calm and well.

I sat for another ten minutes, watching my surroundings and listening to the dark silence, and sipped my wine occasionally as the minutes soldiered slowly along to the twenty-minute mark. Everything was quiet, save only the ticking of a clock out in the hallway, making my vigil in this portion of the mansion uneventful thus far.

> 11:37 PM: Still in the dining room. Made a brief foray into the adjacent bedroom, where the psychic Kristy Robinett was said to have encountered the spirit of a ghost claiming it "was embalmed here." The garage on the property was actually used at one time for embalming, back around the time the primary building here served as an osteopathic sanitarium.

I continued my note taking, waiting for the chance occurrence of something extraordinary; however, tonight it seemed the ghosts of Reynolds Mansion were being timid, for whatever reason. Had I made them uncomfortable, I wondered? Could it be that my presence here seemed like an intrusion, and did the otherworldly residents resent my lounging around after dark like this? I began to consider the possibility—however remote it seemed—and eventually settled on offering a mea culpa, of sorts, in the event that I had interfered with anyone's plans for the evening.

"I hope my visit here comes as no disturbance to anyone who may be here," I whispered aloud. "I only wish to observe, and I'll be gone in the morning. Just observing, that's all."

I waited a few seconds, and then added, "but if anyone here would care to allow their presence to be known, I would invite the opportunity to see you."

There was nothing but silence for several more seconds, and at that time I must have considered that my best efforts at establishing friendly contact with any of the Reynolds ghosts had fallen on deaf ears. Then, at precisely 11:41 PM, there was a very loud, obvious *thump* that came from directly behind me, in the direction of the kitchen area. I turned and glanced back, almost expecting to see a cat or other animal come wandering out after leaping from the kitchen counter; but of course, no such animal had been present at all. I rose slowly from my chair, and moving very quietly, I entered the kitchen to see if the source of the loud noise might become apparent. Of course, no culprit had appeared or made its presence known, and as before, I stood alone in a room that seemed unrepentant for withholding its secrets from me.

Completing my investigation, I left the kitchen unsatisfied, and proceeded on through the dining room toward the library. There in the hallway, I paused by the staircase, where the women visiting several months ago had said they'd seen the mysterious young girl that occasionally haunted the mansion's rooms in pensive disquiet. I stood and gazed toward the landing, above which a beautiful painting of Vivien Leigh as Scarlett O'Hara hung on the wall, illuminated only by the soft decorative lights from the banister nearby. This image was a favorite of mine, as it had been rendered from a promotional photo of Leigh that managed to capture an inviting expression, rather than the expected surliness Scarlett O'Hara had been known for. As I stood staring into Leigh's bluish gaze, I imagined the mansion's most enigmatic little shade resembling the actress, just as she had appeared in *Gone With The Wind*, with qualities both charming and unpredictable, tempered somewhat with a youthful vanity and slight brusque.

Lingering for a moment longer, I allowed my eyes to drift upward beyond where I imagined seeing the Lady of Reynolds, following the stairs as they climbed their way along the wall toward the second floor. The crafted railings and molded hand rails were fitted along precisely turned newels as the staircase made its angular path around the landing where Leigh's likeness adorned the wall, leading up into the darkness of the second floor. For an instant, my thoughts dawdled on the prospect of what awaited me there a few hours from now; further on up those stairs, my inquiries into this house's peculiarities would resolve, at least for one evening.

Entering the library, I moved over into one of the leather armchairs in the corner, where I could observe the entire room. This had become my favorite location throughout the entire place, as it evoked a peculiar irony, especially on account of the painting of Barnabas Collins that stared down from the wall. I marveled at the artist's masterful presentation; Jonathan Frid's jaw line and prominent cheekbones were as sharp and cruel as ever. By all accounts, the painting had done well in capturing the actor's stately portrayal of Colinwood's infamous vampire, as well as the cool, mesmeric stare his character often delivered. Above his grave expression was the famous Regency era Brutus haircut Frid wore for the role, complete with the spiky bangs swept forward onto the forehead, suggestive of both the character's vampiric essence as well as his subtle, neoclassical persona.

At some point while I had been stationed here in the library, admiring the eldritch artwork above the bookcase, I managed to glance at my timepiece; it appeared the witching hour had managed to sneak up on me, and it was now just after midnight.

12:03 AM: Spent the last 15 minutes in the library... nothing eventful here, save the clocks, bells, and chimes around the room that continue to want to interact with me somehow. It is a curious sensation here, indeed.

The comfort of the leather chair I was resting in, along with the hypnotic chiming of animated bells and ancient chimes in the clocks and other trinkets that decorated the room, had now threatened to betray my will to remain awake and alert during my nighttime vigil. I had begun to feel an urge to move away from the comfort this study provided, and soon relented in taking my operation across the hallway to the parlor.

As one enters this room, there is an immediate sense of comfort and cordiality, though there is also an intrigue that the parlor boasts that sets it aside from the other rooms at Reynolds Mansion. A fireplace on the far right wall faces an inviting conversation area, and antique cushioned furniture is spaced throughout the rest of the room. By the window adjacent to the doorway one will find an ornate server, complete with a modest selection of fine bottled spirits that are always kept on hand, and

Senator Robert Reynolds' official portrait

opposite this in the corner left of the parlor hangs the official portrait of Senator Bob Reynolds, who lived here for parts of his tenure in Washington. During his lifetime, Reynolds would try his hand at a wide and unusual range of professions, from wrestler and film producer to reporter and, of course, politician. Leaning forward, cigarette in hand, his portrait shows the Senator with an almost concerned expression on his face, as the Capital Building looms in the distance against an orange sky.

But by far the most alluring element within this room is the portrait of Evalyn Washington McLean, young bride and late wife of the Senator, which hangs above the bar. Despite her wealth, Evalyn had lived a troubled existence, and succeeded in taking her own life—following several failed attempts—by the time she was just twenty-four. The painting, reproduced from a framed photograph now displayed in the hallway, is a beautiful rendering of the youth in all her vibrant and tragic essence. She is stately and elegant, with a grace unmatched that resides amidst her glowing character. Her blond hair flows and curls in waves along her rounded chin, enveloping red lips that invite a longing from within the recesses of the heart, and yet working all the while to conceal a secret diffidence betrayed by the girl's deep, amber eyes. Calm and lovely, Evalyn rests her gaze someplace well outside the concerns of those who stop here to admire her beauty; and of course, the jeweled necklace that once bore the famous Hope Diamond meanders along the snowfall of her neck and shoulders, bringing the famous and foreboding stone to rest along the gentle slopes of her breast.

I stood gazing into Evalyn's portrait, and my mind slowly eased itself into her static world, contained within the frame's four edges. I found myself imagining how that haunted stone will remain here forever, in a sense. Within the subdued brushstrokes that fill the canvas, it will rest eternally on the fair skin of the only beauty to ever match its allure. She too had been discovered in the rough, and like her jewel, she had been hardened somehow to match the stone that carried her burden. Here now, and forever on the canvas, Evalyn's beauty could overshadow all the world's finest wealth and brilliance.

After lingering a while in the parlor, it became evident that my first evening wandering alone through the halls of Reynolds Mansion was steadily resolving. My eyelids had become heavier as I sat here in the room where Evalyn and Robert's likenesses slow danced to imaginary waltzes by night, and I finally decided to make Maggie's Room—understood to be one of the mansion's most haunted guest rooms—my final destination for the evening.

During my ascent, I stopped and looked for a moment out the second story balcony windows overlooking the landscape below. The mountain and surrounding area has changed in a drastic way since Daniel Reynolds first came to build here more than 150 years ago; the once prosperous landscape that boasted livestock, wheat, and corn spanning 250 acres of cultivated property now serves as the site for a new development, with several stories of apartments stacked in buildings that line the streets, leading into a central commerce area replete with shops, restaurants, boutiques, and even fitness clubs. In the distance, parts of Asheville's metro rise above the tree line, and if one listens carefully, the occasional rumble of traffic will drift across the valley, courtesy of the late night tractor-trailers that barrel along the highway towards town. It becomes hard to imagine, seeing all this as it is now, that Asheville's population had barely exceeded 500 residents when Colonel Daniel came here to settle and tend his farmland. Today, the old Reynolds family home remains in that spot on the hill that Daniel once visited long ago; like an elderly grandfather overlooking the family that has all but forgotten him, he watches as they grow into adulthood, forging ahead and leading new lives... all the while losing aspects of their youthful past to the speed of modernization and prosperity.

The third floor staircase viewed from outside Maggie's Room

It was nearing one o'clock as I reached the top of the final staircase. Entering Maggie's room, I locked the door behind me, opened the curtains on the windows to allow the moonlight into the room, and turned off the air conditioner by the far wall. I didn't even bother to change into my nightclothes; I only kicked off my shoes and fell over onto the bed, prepared to go dodging out into the hall should any odd or suspicious sounds happen to interrupt my night's rest. Sleep would soon follow, with any luck, and my final thoughts before my intended rest had been of the chair by the closet door: I imagined it becoming animate, dragging itself over by the bed to observe the intruder lying beneath its covers.

The bed was soft and comfortable—no doubt more comfortable than the beds that existed here in the days when Annie

Lee ran about as a youth—and yet, despite the drowsiness that was setting in, I wasn't finding an occasion for restfulness. Though very tired, I wavered for what seemed like hours on the mere verge of sleep, going through desperate motions with eyes closed, but never able to lapse into a decent slumber. What seemed like every half hour or so, I would come fully awake with a violent start; at one point, I couldn't have been more certain that a small hand had grasped at my ankles, tugging light and quick as if to say, "sleep is not for you… not on this night!" Had I been dreaming, or perhaps merely relenting to a far greater desire to meet this young girl than I even realized?

Sitting up in bed, my attention immediately fell on the chair by the closet door, which remained just where it had been when I first came into the room hours earlier. I noticed I was sweating badly at this point, and the few fleeting moments I had managed to drift within sight of Nod's land of slumber had each resulted in abrupt departure. Persistent dreams of a dancing child, leaping onto the bed with exuberance and determination that this weary interloper would remain awake until the morning, had haunted me far worse than any ghost ever might have done. How I wished I could awaken to find her there, resting in the chair by the bed, ready for conversation at an inopportune hour; perhaps then I would learn what forces, aside from the workings of my own imagination, were conspiring to see that my night here in Maggie's Room would be a restless one.

When morning did finally arrive, I found no use in struggling on with attempts at sleep any longer. The promise of a well-prepared breakfast awaiting me downstairs had been enough incentive to get me out of bed already, and before long I had showered, grabbed my sport coat and begun my descent along the staircase, observing the mansion's various rooms as the soft light of morning cast each one in slightly different roles from the night before. I was amazed at how different this place could seem at times, relative only to the hour of the day, and perhaps the company in residence at any given time. It was as though each part of the building had been capable of wearing masks of opportunity whenever they chose, at times disguising themselves from those who entered; while at others they would seem to allow stark essences of secrets kept within to pour through with an almost reckless abandon.

I stopped long enough to make a cup of coffee on the second floor as I made my way downstairs, selecting one from the variety of coffees and teas Billy kept next to Keurig single-cup brewers on each level of the house. As my coffee was brewing, the only other people who had been staying at Reynolds Mansion that weekend, a middle-aged husband and wife from Kentucky, came out of their room and strolled by on their way to breakfast. I gave them a cheerful salute, hoping there were no dark circles under my eyes that might cause them to mistake me for the kind of otherworldly quarry I'd been seeking the night before. Only moments later, coffee in hand, I made my way downstairs and entered the dining room, where Billy had saved a place for me at the head of the table.

"Here Micah, have a seat," he said welcoming me, grabbing the nearly full cup of coffee from my hands. "We'll warm that up for you too."

The breakfast that followed was choice; a cool and tangy fruit salad, followed by fresh warm crêpes served with bananas, nuts, and a mildly sweet sausage. The coffee that replaced my brew from upstairs had been a special variety, to which Billy added a select amount of spices that gave it a wintery appeal. As I sat talking with the other guests over breakfast, Billy told them I was a writer.

"So do you write novels?" The husband asked.

"Well, I don't count on my fiction very much these days. I'm primarily a journalist, though my areas of expertise are a bit unique. Science stuff, mostly."

"He writes about ghosts too," Billy interjected. "There sure are enough of them around here. So maybe when you visit, they'll end up helping you find new inspiration."

The couple seemed interested in all this, and we continued to chat until they were ready to head into town for the afternoon. Our host and I recommended a few local attractions and restaurants they might try, and as they were leaving, I thanked Billy for his hospitality, and the fancy breakfast. His interest had been with regard to other matters, however.

"So you didn't see any ghosts last night?" Billy asked.

"Well, I can't say I saw any this time. If there were ghosts, they were far more interested in keeping me awake than they were intent on being seen."

The circumstances that brought Billy Sanders and Michael Griffith to Reynolds Mansion had been opportune, if not serendipitous. Their first visit to the site had been in August of 2009, at which time Michael's aunt Claudette, who had also been their realtor, accompanied them. The building had been in a state

Billy Sanders (left) and Michael Griffith

of mild disarray during their initial visit, having served as a well-established bed and breakfast for close to twenty years. Mrs. Helen Faber, who purchased the home with her husband Fred in 1970, had finally decided to sell the mansion after five years in business that followed Fred's passing. During their time here, the place underwent extensive restorations, combating damage from rainwater and general neglect that resulted in a multitude of problems throughout parts of the building. Together, the Fabers reopened the home as The Old Reynolds Mansion, taking its first incarnation as a bed and breakfast within two years of their purchase. The mansion saw various minor renovations and additions during the years that the Fabers owned it (mostly the inclusion of new bathrooms to meet the need of guests). Together, the couple would continue to operate the building for the next three decades, until Fred fell ill and passed away in late June of 2003. Not one to submit even in the absence of her husband, Mrs. Faber hoped to soldier on with the help of family members, though the Old Reynolds Mansion Bed and Breakfast would barely remain in operation for a number of years, before Sanders and Griffith eventually discovered it in August of 2009.

"I remember looking up at the beautiful brick house perched on top of this ridge at the foothill of Reynolds Mountain," Sanders said. "It was at that moment, I knew that this was the one, that this would be where we would live." In October, the sale was finalized, and by April of 2010 the bed and breakfast would be fully restored and operational once again. But there had been other circumstances that surrounded the decision to purchase the place, as well. In fact, Billy conceded that just prior to making final their decision to purchase Reynolds Mansion, he and Michael had even consulted with a longtime friend and neighbor named Jen, whose reputation for being gifted with unique powers of intuition and otherworldly insight ended up proving very worthwhile.

"While we were living in Chicago, Jen was our neighbor, and she was a psychic, although Michael and I were always kind of skeptical," Billy explained. "When Michael and I first decided to buy a bed and breakfast, we didn't tell anyone, but we decided we would ask her thoughts on things. She, Michael and I were having dinner one night, and I told her I just wanted her impression about something. There were four bed and breakfasts we had looked at, three that were already running and making a profit. Then there was Reynolds Mansion, even in its poor state at the time, which was among the photos we showed her.

"We had made up our mind already which one we would be investing in, during our flight back from Asheville to Chicago. However, Michael wanted to test Jen, so when we were having dinner, we began by showing her photos of several locations in the area that we had kept in mind. She looked at each photograph, occasionally running her hands over them, palms faced downward, and telling us things about each location. 'No, you don't want this one,' or maybe she'd say something about the energy she felt on this one. 'This one is not what it seems,' she told us of another. Then she got to Reynolds Mansion, and said immediately, 'this one has a different feeling. And there *are* ghosts here, but it doesn't feel like a negative energy. There is a spirit on the third floor, but it's a good one.' She seemed taken with it, despite the bad condition of the building," Bill remembered. Then, at that moment, and very suddenly, she had looked up at Billy and Michael with a curious gaze.

"Are you thinking about turning this into a bed and breakfast?"

As recent history now shows, the two had indeed been contemplating a purchase, with interest in staking their own claim in the Asheville bed and breakfast scene. Had they only known how well their hard work and diligence in restoring the building would pay off, they might have been surprised indeed; within the first few months following the reopening of Reynolds Mansion to the public, the location began to receive top ranking at TripAdvisor.com, a website that assists people in gathering travel information about accommodations and other useful data for locations they plan to visit. Reynolds Mansion not only ranked number one among bed and breakfasts in the Asheville area, but second in the entire nation, and among the top twelve worldwide. But while the future of Reynolds Mansion, based on the fame and appeal it had begun to garner, seemed bright and certain, I found that a desire to unravel it's curious past—much of which remained shrouded in mystery—had begun to consume my thoughts following that first night spent in Maggie's Room. What had initially amounted to being a friend's catering to my professional interest in the paranormal had now grown into a strange and insatiable passion. What, exactly, was it about this place that haunted me so? Despite all the curious stories, the marvelous wealth, and the decades upon decades of life and living that had occurred here, I had somehow been taken with something else the building seemed desperate to offer. Indeed, there was mystery to be unraveled here, and long forgotten passions that had never seen fulfillment. There were lingering echoes of good times long gone, and bad times hardly forgotten; it all amounted to there being an incredible energy about the place; at times I would find it both terrific and terrifying.

But despite this, nothing about Reynolds Mansion could be called unsettling, and in lieu of having any earthly aptitudes for sensing the spirit realm that I knew of at the time, it was apparent after my introduction to the place that I must become far better acquainted with this old house and its mysteries. Whatever it was that had been longed for here, perhaps it was what had kept the mansion's illustrious ghosts around for so long, too. Perhaps this same energy had now drawn me into its madness also, like the proverbial moth that flies longingly into the flame that will eventually consume him. Whatever the case, for good or for ill, a part of me remained within the mansion already, and whatever results might turn up at some point ensuing, I no longer had any choice but to attempt to find out what about this ancient home had managed to drag me into the epicenter of its yearning intrigue.

.

Three

PARALLELS TO THE PAST

"The past and the present have intermingled at Collinwood, and the ancestral home has become a source of strange occurrences and strong curiosities. A foreboding structure can attract the least suspecting."

DARK SHADOWS, EPISODE 222, AIRED 3 MAY 1967

EVERY STORY MUST HAVE ITS BEGINNINGS TUCKED AWAY someplace, and as the author and protagonist Ben Mears said in King's *Salem's Lot*, "from such inconsequential beginnings, dynasties have been built." Truer words, perhaps, were never spoken, and so far as the building of Reynolds Mansion is concerned, the beginnings of this illustrious tale have their origins across the great waters of the Atlantic, beginning in Medieval England in the 1600s near West Sussex, in an area called Chichester.

One of the great and ancient cathedral cities of the historic County of Sussex, Chichester—or *Chiddester* as allowed according to the local dialect—houses many of Great Britain's oldest churches and buildings, including a 12th century cathedral that still exists today. It was in this town, existing now as a transportation hub and political stronghold throughout the region, that William Reynolds settled and met his future wife, Margaret Exton. The two were married on March 6, 1644 at the same ancient stone chapel where Margaret had been baptized 19 years earlier, known as the St Pancras Church. In use since A.D. 314, St Pancras is believed to be one of the oldest places of Christian worship in all of England. It

The Old Saint Pancras Church, image by Justin Cormack

owes its namesake to the Roman martyr who was beheaded near the chapel site at age fourteen, having professed his faith only a decade prior to the stone church being erected at the site in his honor. In truth, the name of St Pancras would eventually be applied to the entire surrounding parish jurisdiction; running close to Regent's Park in the west, and toward the east along a road known today as York Way. These days, Oxford Street would form the seat of what had once been the southern end of the old parish, and finally, running north as far as Highgate, the purported home of a legendary vampire within the North London town's famous cemetery.

William Reynolds never immigrated to the New World, though at least one of his sons, Henry, would eventually cross the great proverbial pond to start a new life, spending twenty-two weeks in transit across the Atlantic Ocean in 1676. He stayed in Burlington, New Jersey for a time after arriving, and eventually met his bride, Prudence Clayton, whom he married on November 10, 1678. The new Reynolds family eventually settled in Chester County, Pennsylvania, though Henry maintained ownership of some of the family's land overseas in parts of Chichester and Nottingham. Only four years prior to his death, Henry famously established a stone tavern, intended to serve as a stage stop, on lot number 17 on the western end of an 18,000 acre tract of land purchased in 1701 by William Penn called the Nottingham Lots. Over the entrance of Reynolds' tavern was said to be a swinging sign, inscribed with lettering that read "THE RISING SUN," with rays beaming outward that resembled the morning sky at dawn.

With time, an entire village would begin to form around Henry's public house, with the locality eventually receiving the name of Summer Hill. But despite the commerce growing around it, the tavern itself had seemed to remain central to all things in the township; it began to grow a reputation for being a popular gathering place, used for such things as political meetings and elections, business deals, and a variety of other events and gatherings in the Summer Hill community. With time, "We'll meet at the Rising Sun" was a common saying used throughout the region, marking the location as a hub central not only to the physical locality, but to the hearts and minds of all those who traversed it. By 1815, once the town had incorporated its first post office (operated, in all likelihood, from within the very stone walls of Henry's own tavern), the name "Summer Hill" had fallen away in favor of Rising Sun for the town's new official name; it remains as such to this day.

Prudence bore Henry eight children—four boys and four girls—during their years together, and following Henry's death on August 7, 1724, Prudence was left "all goods and personal estate," according to her late husband's will. To his son Francis, he left his plantation of 290 acres, that still existed near the family home back at Chichester; his son John received 210 acres of the Chichester land, with each of the boys receiving additional instruction to pay their youngest brother, William, a sum of 20 pounds on the day of his twenty-first birthday. Another sibling, Henry, was given a tract of land in Nottingham consisting of 490 acres, and young William would obtain an equal measure of the Nottingham property. Once the land and wealth had been divided among his sons, Henry's daughters—Margaret, Prudence, Deborah, and Hannah, all of whom had married by this time—were each left a sum of one shilling.

Young William Reynolds had been born on July 5, 1701 to Henry and Prudence at their Chester County home in Pennsylvania. On January 23, 1723, he was married to Mary Brown, just one year prior to his father's passing. William remained with

Mary until her death fifteen years later on January 19, 1739, and following Mary's passing, Reynolds would take a second wife only a few months later in October of that same year, marrying seventeen-year-old Rachel John. Between the two marriages, William Reynolds had more than ten children; he and Mary had given birth to Samuel, Ishman, Jeremiah, David, John David, Catherine, Hannah, Jonathan, Mary, and William Reynolds. His subsequent marriage to Rachel John resulted in the birth of four more children, according to available genealogical data: their names were Henry, Rachel, Solomon, and a second son bearing the name John.

Of all the men in the Reynolds lineage, William could well have been the first to relocate to North Carolina, where he would remain until his death on June 29, 1773 at the age of 71. One of William's sons by Mary, John David Reynolds, would also come to reside in the Rip Van Winkle State, settling in Guilford County, where his parents had lived, though also maintaining ties to parts of states to the North as well. Among these were areas around Bedford and Amherst Counties in Virginia; while the 1810 census lists John Reynolds' residence as being in Guilford County, North Carolina, there is also a John Reynolds that shows up within listings for the aforementioned Bedford County. This could have been one of the sons of John Daniel (as he was known to have sons by the names of both John and Jonathon by his wife, Mary Parker), and this thus supports a necessary link between another of John Daniel's sons, Abraham Reynolds, and his birthplace in Amherst County, Virginia.

While this should seem far less an item of controversy than portrayed here at present, sources published in Buncombe County, North Carolina around 1981 state that Abraham Reynolds—the original Reynolds to settle in the Asheville area—had been born in

Maryland. While a few sources still cite this information, nearly all of them can be traced back to the 1981 book published by The Old Buncombe County Genealogical Society titled *The Heritage of Old Buncombe County, Volume I.* (This same book cites the month of death for Abraham's ancestor and co-founder of Rising Sun, Henry Reynolds, as having been in October; despite the fact that his will was probated in August of that same year, prior to when he supposedly died!) According to genealogical information available elsewhere, borrowing information that has been cross-referenced with a number of family trees that incorporate the early Reynolds ancestors, we begin to see that a very different story emerges: based on the family's aforementioned ties to parts of middle and southern Virginia, far more credence can be afforded the numerous accounts that exist which place Abraham's birth in Amherst County, Virginia. On the other hand few, if any, seem to link the family back to Maryland, as had been previously suggested.

Regardless of the birthplace controversy, the family of Abraham Reynolds was said to have eventually moved to Rowan County, North Carolina, where Abraham would meet his future wife, Mary Leazer, who he married in 1796. The following year, Morristown, county seat of Buncombe County, where the newlyweds Abraham and Mary would relocate, was incorporated and renamed Asheville. Abraham went on to claim seven land grants from the State of North Carolina, completing a tract of land totaling 1,575 acres south of Asheville along Bent Creek, where he and Mary would settle and begin raising their family. The state grant for Tract Number 43 had been issued to Reynolds in 1800, and within five years, he managed to clear about 15.5 acres of the property, which also contained what is known as the old Daniel Boone Lake site. Parts of the property were farmed and maintained until well after Reynold's death, seeing produce as recently as the 1930s. In fact, the land was still described as being "in good condition" for farming when it was sold to wealthy businessman George Vanderbilt in 1900.

During the Reynolds years there at Bent Creek, a rustic agricultural approach had been a way of life, and the family of Abraham Reynolds worked the land in this manner during their entire time spent there. Though Abraham would nearly live to see his son's construction of a large new home on a mountainside north of Asheville, his beloved Mary passed away on September 17, 1813 at the young age of 38. In all likelihood, this resulted from complications following the birth of her youngest daughter, Barbara, who had been delivered only three days earlier. Abraham would continue on after Mary's passing for another three decades; he eventually died on November 3, 1846 at the age of 78; within one year of the construction of Reynolds Mansion. Abraham and Mary are buried together in the family cemetery that still exists near the Bent Creek home site.

❖ ❖ ❖

Of that aforementioned Reynolds son, whose dreams of settling north of Asheville have come to our attention already, much can be said indeed. Daniel Reynolds, who later in life would construct the large residence known today as Reynolds Mansion, was born at the Reynolds family home site at Bent Creek on March

Daniel Reynolds, whose portrait (above) adorns the wall at Reynolds Mansion

20, 1809. As Abraham and Mary's youngest son, he had grown up helping tend his father's large tracts of land in the area, and by the time he had reached his early twenties, Daniel left to work as a commissioned officer, serving as ensign to a company designed to assist with the Indian movement that had been underway. The group marched as far west as Bryson City, but within thirty days the operation returned to Buncombe County and disbanded.

Daniel, who would go on to take the nickname "Colonel," would continue working farming jobs, and in the early 1840's, he accepted a position of employ under farmer Israel Baird, who owned and operated an 800-acre area of farmland two miles north of downtown Asheville. Baird's property encompassed the entire area known today as Beaver Lake, and Daniel's position had been primarily as an overseer for Baird's farm; it was also while working here that Reynolds first met his employer's daughter, Susan Adelia

The Sons of Daniel Reynolds

Baird. The two grew fond of one another, and were soon married on October 7, 1844 in a ceremony officiated by Daniel's older brother, the travelling Reverend John Reynolds. As a gift, Susan's father granted the newlyweds 1500 acres of land on a mountain nearby, which overlooked his farming operation in the valley, as well as parts of the "Baird Bottoms" near Beaver Lake, which those living in the area called it. At the time of the 1850 Census, Daniel Reynolds had still been listed professionally as a farmer, with the total value of his real estate at about $6,500.

Ten children were eventually born between Daniel and Susan Reynolds, five boys and five girls. Watching his family grow, Reynolds— always the entrepreneur,

Susan (center) and her surviving daughters

and wanting to provide for them—made the decision to steer away from farming life and the Baird operation north of town. Within just a few years, he managed to obtain both a mail contract and a stagecoach line, which began its route over in Rowan County in the town of Salisbury. Heading west through Morganton, the coach would continue its way up the mountain back toward Asheville, where it would then retrace its course for a new line of passengers awaiting it here in the mountains.

The stagecoach line and mail delivery services had already grounded Reynolds in the burgeoning mountain town as a purveyor of transportation and communication services, but even gaining a handle on these key industries hadn't seemed to quell his desire for creating opportunities, and thus his involvement in a variety of industries would continue (this would be a tendency shared by a number of his ancestors later on, just as well). Reynolds would also claim the title of hotelkeeper, beginning a new operation over in town; and not to be outdone, following the family's long-standing adherence to God's word, Daniel, like his elder brother John, was also ordained to the Methodist Church.

Reynolds would oversee these various operations until well into the 1850's, when he sold many of them off, acquiring some land near Baird Bottoms with intention of farming and apple growing. Though the latter would serve as his last profession in life, it would hardly become that for which he was best remembered. Indeed, by the late 1840s Daniel Reynolds had also begun to show an interest in politics, and was successfully elected to a one-year term as Buncombe County Trustee in 1850. The short time spent in public service served in whetting Reynolds' appetite for holding a position in office, and four years later, he would challenge his bride's cousin, Zebulon Baird Vance, for a seat in the North Carolina House of Commons.

Between the two men, differences were primarily few: both were Whigs, supporting urbanization and industrialization in the Asheville area, as well as keeping tariffs and other protectionist sentiments central to their philosophies. Even on a state level, the two contenders had agreed on perhaps a majority of the issues central to the election. However, their primary point of difference had been a great one, and one of key importance in a Southern State like North Carolina: how to deal with the issue of slavery. Vance accepted the Compromise of 1850, a series of bills later credited with having played a major role toward staving off secession, and thus postponing the Civil War for a decade (in midst of controversial provisions such as the Fugitive Slave Act, which the Compromise also included). Reynolds, on the opposite ideological extreme, argued in favor of the divisive Kansas-Nebraska Act, issued earlier that election year by Stephen Douglas. The act had been intended to repeal the Congress's earlier Missouri Compromise, spurring directly the formation of a new political party that called themselves Republicans; within ten years, their sweeping capture of the national government in 1860 would break the veritable dam that held back secession's strong floodwaters.

The contention between the candidates and their political views toward the slavery issue resulted in a heated campaign, from which Vance would emerge the clear victor. While Reynolds had managed to secure 579 votes, this only amounted to 46% of the vote needed to take the county; Vance managed to carry nine of the county's eleven precincts, drawing a winning turnout that totaled 688 votes cast, beating Reynolds by a fair margin.

Reynolds finally seemed cured of his political aspirations after this, and following his electoral defeat by future governor Vance, he retired to his land near the Baird Bottoms to the north of town, where he sought to tap his old roots of farming and reinvent himself, yet again, this time as an apple grower. Reynolds built an earthen dam for the waterway that would eventually be christened Beaver Lake, operating a gristmill and water-powered saw mill along the site. Additionally, toward the east end of the lake existed a clay pit, from which the Reynolds family operated a small brickyard.

This source of good red clay had been integral not only to various infrastructure in the early Asheville area, but also to the construction of Reynolds's own home, which stood on the nearby mountain that bore his namesake. Building was officially undertaken of the federal-style house by 1847, following Daniel's purchase of 488 acres of land at public auction. The design of this illustrious home was the kind reserved only to Asheville' wealthiest in those years preceding the Civil War, a time during which contractor Ephram Clayton had been particularly active in the area. Though few records exist to substantiate his involvement in the design of Reynold's home, it seems likely for that time—and for a man of Daniel Reynolds' prosperity and prestige—that Clayton would have been hired for the job.

Reynolds put the fifteen slaves that he owned to work constructing the home, following a double-pile plan as the bricks that formed its massive foundation were laid. Once completed, the new Reynolds family home stood as a two-story building with internal chimneys, hipped roof and the customary single porch that ran along the house's front end, finalizing the building's balanced and symmetrical look through popular Federal styling (and despite how the period coinciding with the building's eponymous construction style had officially ended nearly two decades earlier).

At the time Daniel and his family had taken residence at the new home, Asheville still remained a fairly small mountain town. A meager population of 520 existed within the town area, which included 86 slaves and six free blacks. Much like Reynolds' own aspirations would drive him toward transportation of goods and services, one of the region's major commerce routes, the Buncombe Turnpike, also passed directly through the area, making the Reynolds farmland key to further prosperity in the region. From his stronghold less than four miles from Asheville, Reynolds was able to oversee the raising of livestock on his farmland, as well as the harvest of wheat and corn in large quantities. At one time, the cash value of the Reynolds farm alone had tallied $8,000, with the value of his personal estate coming in at an additional $18,000.

As the saying goes, however, all things must pass, and sadly, once the disquiet of a nation torn had begun to sweep across the southern hills and valleys, bringing the sort of eventual change that would accompany the American Civil War, the otherwise prosperous land surrounding Reynolds' luxurious mountain home had lost a tremendous amount of its value. By the late 1870s, Daniel Reynolds' estate had been stripped to a mere shell of its former self, with the primary home tract of 140 acres being all that remained. The total value of the property was estimated at just $1000 at the time of Reynolds' death on January 21, 1878.

When Daniel Reynolds passed away, his son, William Taswell Reynolds, then twenty-nine years old, was called into administration of his late father's estate, which he officially bought sometime between 1885 and 1887. At age thirty-one, he married Mary Elizabeth Spears in October of 1880, and despite owning his father's spacious home, he and Mary (who preferred the nickname "Mamie") chose to reside on Woodfin Street in town the majority of their time together. Thus, Reynolds Mansion would eventually end up changing hands again, once William sold it to his younger brother, Nathaniel Augustus Reynolds, in 1890.

William was described as being an "energetic and progressive citizen," who, like his father, worked as a hotel owner, tobacco warehouseman, built and managed an opera house on Patton Avenue, and even owned a livery stable on Water Street. Colonel Daniel's appeal for public office had also carried over to William, who served a variety of city and county positions throughout his life. In 1879 William was appointed Tax Collector and Marshall for the City, going on to serve as Alderman five years later. He resigned from this post after one year, to take the position of Clerk of the Superior Court for Buncombe County. He was successfully reelected to this position in 1886, and in another five years he chose to return again to his position as Alderman; a very successful reelection would ensue. Having reclaimed for a second time his earlier position in office, it was while serving again as Alderman that William Reynolds passed away on January 16, 1892. He was only forty-two years old.

Historical records describe William Taswell Reynolds as a man of particular integrity and honest character, willing to sacrifice if necessary to assist friends and family who were less fortunate than he. No doubt, his caring attitude would have reflected on his family at the time of his passing, though William did not manage to prepare any sort of a will, having died at an early age. Also, despite his good character and multiple business endeavors around Asheville, William had also been heavily in debt at the time of his death, and thus the settlement of his estate became a long, tiring ordeal that lasted several years. As a result of many of William's debts needing to be honored, it became necessary for the family home of Colonel Daniel Reynolds to be sold at public auction in 1895. However, the highest bidder in the sale had been none other than William's widow, thirty-three-year-old Mamie Spears Reynolds.

Mamie would nonetheless encounter some difficulty with full acquisition of the estate, regardless of her widowed status, due to the conventions of the time regarding female ownership of property. However, Mamie was not the only widow in the Reynolds family at the time; her brother-in-law Nathaniel (who for a short time had owned the Reynolds house several years earlier), remained unmarried also, following the tragic passing of his young wife, Blanch Vivian. After leaving this world at the otherwise spritely age of twenty, Blanch's passing had been particularly difficult for Nathaniel, who entered a period of mourning that eventually led into real estate development and public service for a period of twelve years. Thus, within a few years of William's passing, Nathaniel and his widowed sister-in-law, Mamie, would eventually marry. Closing the strange gap that existed within the family after the unseasonable deaths of each widow's former spouse, this circumstance also allowed Mamie, having taken a new husband, an opportunity to affirm her acquisition of the old Reynolds property.

And yet, somewhat surprisingly, Mamie and Nathaniel continued living primarily at the residence on Woodfin Street over in town, making little use of the mountain home overlooking the Baird Bottoms. The property, after all, had languished somewhat during the reconstruction era, which occurred mostly during the final years that her deceased father-in-law had owned the place. Things would remain this way until 1904, when Nathaniel, having maintained a particular fondness for the home where he had been raised, made arrangements with Mamie to secure payment of an existing mortgage on the house, thus granting him full, unencumbered ownership of the building and its property.

❖   ❖   ❖

Having served as Justice of the Peace in Buncombe County for a number of years, Nathaniel carried a reputation that was both favorable and consistent in the public eye. Early on, he had attended the University of North Carolina at Chapel Hill, where he undertook two year's study of Law preceding a stint working in the railroad industry. Therefore, by 1913 when the failing health of Erwin W. Patton required him to resign from the Board of County Commissioners, Nathaniel Reynolds seemed a likely man to fill the void; he was quickly sworn in as Chairman of the Buncombe County Board of County Commissioners, a position for which he was well-received. During his tenure, Nathaniel would go on to authorize the concrete paving of a highway from Asheville to Weaverville; additionally, he was well-loved for there being no increase in public debt or sale of bonds during his years serving Buncombe County.

And yet, despite Nathaniel's many exploits and interests, perhaps the one of greatest relevance to us here had been that which involved his father's home. Even after securing ownership of the house in 1904, Nathaniel's love for the Reynolds house hadn't been enough to cement his residence at the site. In fact, before it would eventually become the final place of residence for he and Mamie, the building would yet undergo a number of other curious incarnations that ranged from boarding house prior to World War I, to it's operation as the Asheville Osteopathic Sanitarium between 1919 and 1924 under Dr. Elizabeth Smith.

Listings for the Asheville Osteopathic Sanitarium do appear within an entry in the 1922 *Official Reference Book of the Press Club of Chicago,* which defines osteopathy as "the science of healing by adjustment of the body tissues through the application of natural laws." At the time, osteopathy was viewed as the first scientific practice to recognize the relationship between body mechanism and health. It can be traced back to nineteenth-century physician Andrew Taylor Still, founder of the first osteopathic medical school in Kirksville, Missouri, who proposed its use as an alternative medical practice as far back as 1874, professing that his own disenchantment with the use of medical drugs had begun decades earlier. "The osteopathic physician is trained through four separate school years of nine months each," the source above would state, "in all branches necessary for correct diagnosis and in all the subjects which are universally recognized as a part of a professional education."

According to information contained within the entry for "osteopathy" in the *Press Club of Chicago* reference book:

> While Osteopathy has achieved legal recognition in practically every State in the Union, its greatest recognition has come from gratified patients, many of whom have been restored to health after failing in their search in many other directions. It may be said that the Osteopathic records of success and its reputation have been reared on the failures of other systems of treatment and diagnosis.

The early successes of Osteopathy were won largely in the field of chronic disease and with patients who had tried about everything else in the therapeutic world. But during the great influenza epidemic of 1918, Osteopathic physicians made such a wonderful record, that Osteopathy achieved at a bound the most widespread recognition in the treatment of this acute malady together with the treatment of the pneumonia which so often followed its onset.

Dr. George W. Riley of New York City collected the statistics of the Osteopathic profession with reference to this epidemic. Out of 110,122 cases of "flu" reported, there were 257 deaths, a mortality % of 1 per cent. The medical death rate was forty times as high. Out of 6,350 cases of epidemic pneumonia reported, there were 635 deaths, a mortality of only 10 per cent. The medical rate was three times as high. These figures were collected with the greatest care under responsible direction.

Under Dr. Smith's tenure while the building had been the Asheville Osteopathic Sanitarium, the Reynolds House served primarily as a clinic for tuberculosis patients. Data and existing records pertaining to the number of individuals that visited the site indicate that it was well trafficked, and in likelihood, this may have been partially due to the widely-held belief that the fresh, clear mountain air around Asheville maintained healing attributes, especially for those afflicted with illness that attacked the respiratory system. Today, the cause of tuberculosis is understood to be the result of infection caused by mycobacterium such as *Mycobacterium tuberculosis*; however, at the time of Dr. Elizabeth Smith's tenure at Reynolds Mansion, the disease was still incurable. Thus, it was very common for tuberculosis patients to visit

Asheville, with hope of benefiting from the inhalation of mountain air and its presumed curative properties.

Dr. Smith's involvement with the building would officially end in 1924, and within one year it was decided that the building would resume its place as home to the existing Reynolds family. Nathaniel began extensive renovations in 1925, and central to these were the inclusion of a steep third floor addition featuring a dormered mansard roof, which was constructed above the main portion of the house. This new floor featured a narrow traverse hallway, from which eight small rooms became accessible. New bathrooms were also installed in various locations throughout the home, and a much larger dining room was created, following the removal of a partition wall that separated the dining area from the original kitchen wing. Along with minor first floor alterations, updated woodwork was fitted throughout the home as well, featuring such architectural embellishments as turned wooden corner guards, broad baseboards along interior walls that featured molded caps, and even narrow chair rails in the style of the Colonial Revival, which would match the eventual addition of elaborate porches on the first and second stories, fitted with Revival-style Tuscan columns and modillion entablatures.

An original nomination form for Reynolds Mansion's inclusion on the National Register of Historic Places was submitted to the United States Department of the Interior in 1978. The document, which still exists among files kept by the DOI, gave the following descriptions of vague clues to the building's early appearance, tucked away carefully beneath Nathaniel Reynolds' meticulous and extensive 1925 renovations:

So thorough was the early twentieth-century renovation of the Reynolds House that one must carefully hunt for the nineteenth-century materials remaining in it other than its stout brick walls. Below its roof structure, which was added this century, most of the building's floor and ceiling framing is original frame-sawn timbers displaying heavy timber joinery. All but a few minor interior partitions on the first and second floors are original load-bearing brick walls although the plaster on them is apparently replacement. Original flooring survives beneath pine flooring added during the renovation. A single mid-nineteenth century four-panel door survived on the kitchen wing until recently when it was retired to an outbuilding.

The outline of an earlier mantel is visible on a second-floor fireplace where the newer (ca. 1905) plaster facing to the firebox has chipped away. Besides the items mentioned above, this ghost mark is the only hint of previous finish materials.

As a result of the thorough nature of the renovations, little evidence—if any—still exists that indicates what the original building, as constructed by Daniel Reynolds in 1847, may have actually resembled. The appearance of the original structure would change drastically following Nathaniel's renovations in 1925, remodeling portions of the house right down to its brick framework. Thus, the building that exists today remains vastly different from the one that appeared on the mountainside during the lifetime of Colonel Daniel Reynolds. And yet, despite the outward cosmetic differences, there are still some things that remain distinctly unchanged, though primarily of an unseen nature. The feelings associated with the various rooms, and the strange essences of family life spanning more than a century, all still seem to reside within the house, and today there is a strong sense of comfort that remains at Reynolds Mansion. The building served as a home, if not a literal refuge at times, for those who came and went over the years; sensing this upon entering, one cannot help but accept a strong sense of veneration and warmth, as though the very stuff of home and harbor echoes from its sturdy walls.

Perhaps this sense of belonging that one feels entering Reynolds Mansion is what helped the place attract so many colorful people over the years, and thus, it remains standing today; though truth be known, it had been advised on a few occasions that the entire structure be demolished, having befallen various states of disarray and neglect over the decades. Such instances, however, are merely smaller parts of grander stories to come, involving a multitude of other individuals who would come and go over the years, each with a different vision as to how the place would continue, and what purpose the elderly walls of the Reynolds home might go on to serve. For us here today, they are only history… but for those who *lived* the many changes Reynolds Mansion has seen, these stories represent the essence of such things as life and living, as well as the pursuit of an American dream of hope, security, and prosperity amidst the changes that become inevitable during the course of any given person's lifetime.

Everything's eventual, as one author put it, and the eventuality of Reynolds Mansion and its enchantment would yet become a subtle, inescapable reality for many wandering souls of the living variety, as well as those already departed from this mortal realm.

HOUNDS AT THE GARDEN GATE

"Help Gods, help saints, help sprites and powers that in the heaven do dwell; Help ye that are aye wont to wail, ye howling hounds of hell."

EDWARD DE VERE, "LOSS OF GOOD NAME," 1576

DARK CLOUDS PEELED AWAY IN FEATHERY STRANDS OF GRAY, creating a ceiling above Reynolds Mansion that moved slowly like smoke blowing across the chimneys protruding from its old roof. The evening sky in its present state cast a delightful gloom over the house and surrounding property, and light raindrops sprinkled over me as Chris Heyes and I emerged from my vehicle, removing equipment from the trunk of my car and carrying it toward the house. The date was January 10, 2012, and the occasion had been a remote broadcast of my weekly Internet radio program, *The Gralien Report*, live from the Reynolds Mansion. Chris, my producer and co-host, helped me carry microphones and other equipment across the wet gravel toward the back door, where Billy would soon appear to greet us. My associate and I welcomed the contrasting warmth of indoors as we entered the building, which was drier in equal measure than the rear parking lot had been, and far more forgiving with regard to the sensitive recording equipment we carried under each arm.

There were no guests staying at Reynolds on this particular evening, and having the entire place to himself, Billy had made sure the rooms of the mansion were sparsely lit, casting them in a soft, eerie light. We followed our host down the hall to the library, and after chatting a while over coffee, Billy cleared a round table in the center of the room, where we began setting up our live broadcasting equipment. It was just under three hours until airtime, and our arrangement slowly began taking the shape of a makeshift studio setup. I found it very fitting that we would be composing our remote recording array on a rounded table in one of the mansion's more atmospheric rooms; after all, what we hoped to perform this evening might be likened to being a sonic séance, of sorts, where dynamic microphones and powered mixers would serve as our metallic mediums to voices and messages from another world.

At one point while setting things up for the broadcast that would ensue later that evening, Billy left the mansion to make a trip to the supermarket. Nearing completion of our on-the-spot audio arrangement, I advised Chris to finish things up while I stepped outside to call Matt Oakley, the board operator and third-wheel of our broadcasting faction. Making my exit into the hallway, I was duly startled to find a person standing there, so close to the doorway that I nearly collided with her! My mind had been racing within the instant; Billy had already gone, and there were no others in the building with us. I was certain the door had been locked behind him on his way out, but who else would have a key…

"Oh, Jess," I said, as the momentary confusion crystallized into familiarity within the instant. "You're lucky I didn't let out an almighty shriek, with you sneaking around like that." Jess was one of the mansion's employees, who lived in a small apartment in the upstairs of the adjacent building overlooking the garden. Chris and I had spoken to her briefly earlier in the evening upon arriving, and armed with a key to the main building, she had now managed to surprise us.

"Looks like I startled you," she said, with a sly grin.

"Had I not known any better," I continued, "I might have thought you were one of the mansion's many lingering specters."

"Well, there are a few of those seen around here from time to time."

"And I'm one who wants to learn all their secrets," I said, reentering the library. "I want to hear everything they have to say, and listen to every one of their little voices in the darkness that come calling out."

"Where did Billy go?" she asked.

"He just went to the store, but I'm sure he'll be back soon. He's going to be joining us on the air at eight."

"He's actually going to be going on your show?" Jess said with a touch of incredulity. "That surprises me, because he and I are a lot alike. Neither of us really likes being around people all that much."

"Come on now, Jess. Billy Sanders is a regular social butterfly when he needs to be," I joked. "And besides, the man has become a dear friend in the short course of my visits to this place. I doubt he feels any need to withhold secrets; whether they deal with spooks that go bump in the night, or the living kind that wander these halls."

"Oh, you'll find out some secrets if you hang around here long enough," Jess said cryptically. Her voice became faint as it trailed off down the hallway, following her departure from the building. Just before she left, we could hear as she murmured some final offering—something barely even audible—that had to do with *secrets*. Though I couldn't discern what she was saying, I had the strangest sensation come over me at that instant, and in this moment of pause, I glanced over at Chris, who had already been looking at me with an odd expression, eyebrows climbing his forehead. Indeed, our sentiments had been mutual regarding the eerie exchange, and without another word, we each went back to our business in silence until the familiar, rusty voice of our engineer became audible through the earpiece of my cell phone.

Within another half hour, Chris and I had arranged all the microphones, laptop computers, mixers and other equipment around the table in the center of the library, creating a modest but functional setup for our live webcast. Soon afterward Matt Oakley also joined us, whose clever on-air quips, dispersed amidst my usual banter with Chris each week, would no doubt lend a touch of levity to the otherwise contemplative nature of the evening's broadcast, centering primarily around our host's recollections about the history of the house. Finally, additional provisions would be allotted for updates regarding news and politics each hour as well; the night of our live broadcast from Reynolds Mansion also happened to coincide with the 2012 New Hampshire GOP Primary.

As we neared airtime, the cold, damp weather had been wreaking havoc with my already fragile vocal chords, following my recovery from what I endearingly referred to as "the cough of Christmas past"; this was merely seasonal lingo for a chest cold that had lingered with me since the holidays, and had carried over well into the New Year. Apparently, Chris had been affected by the same virus, and was busily mixing hot liquid concoctions containing tea blended with lemon juice, honey, and packets of Emergen-C vitamin supplement to try and ward off the ill effects such an affliction can tend to have on one's ability to speak. By the time 8:00 PM Eastern Time had arrived, Matt and Chris were busily gathering news stories, as I fumbled with cables and chords that would feed audio to a laptop nearby that we used to record the program. Finally, the show's theme music began to play, and within moments I could hear the barrel-chested voice of Dick Oakley, our program's announcer, resounding through my earpiece. Soon, we would be sharing our weird evening together at a haunted mansion with listeners all across the continental United States.

"For a change, we're actually broadcasting from another location," I began, cuing our engineer to engage the other microphones. "But I'm still your Mouth of the South, and welcome one and all to The Gralien Report. Another week of wildness— another week of *weirdness*—and here we are, broadcasting to you live from a haunted mansion in Western North Carolina." Indeed, there certainly was a unique excitement in the air.

"We'll be taking questions from you by phone throughout the night for our 'host with the ghost,' Mr. Billy Sanders," I told our listeners. "He was gracious enough to join us here on the program and talk a little about this, so I'd like to begin by asking him this: how does one come into living and taking residence at a place like Reynolds Mansion?"

"Well, I had always known that I would run a bed and breakfast," Billy began. He was cool and comfortable with the microphone, and though picking his words carefully, still managed to sound as though the thoughts being spoken had been said many times before already. "When I started looking, I actually started with bed and breakfasts that were already up and running, and making a profit. When we came across Reynolds Mansion it was, of course, in very bad shape. It had been shut down since about 2003, so there was a lot of restoration work that needed to be done.

"We knew that Reynolds Mansion was haunted when we bought it, because it is in a lot of books, and on the web. I had done some investigation, so I knew it had a history of being haunted. When I saw it for the first time, I knew immediately that it was where I would live, but that also meant that it would be a lot of work. It was actually *seven months* of work; we had three crews working 24 hours a day, seven days a week to complete the restoration on it, and it opened on April 15th of last year.

"You know," Billy said, with a touch of reflection, "having been built in 1847, the number of people that have passed—that have been born, died, and have gone through this house—it's kind of staggering when you start thinking about it. All those people have left a presence here—an energy—and I think sometimes that it kind of permeates back out, for whatever reason."

I shared Billy's latest sentiment, which aroused in my mind another of Victoria Winters' famous quotes of *Dark Shadows* fame; no doubt, this was due in part to my knowledge of Jonathan Frid's eerie portrait, looming from the wall directly behind me:

I believe in a past, and I believe in a present; and I think that sometimes, at some very special moment, they become confused—they meet—and I think that, perhaps, tonight was one of those nights.

Following the program's opening segment, we spent the majority of our time throughout the course of the next two hours having Billy recount several of the mansion's odd and alluring tales of ghosts and strange happenings. We discussed the visit from psychic-intuitive Kristy Robinett, and her story of a young girl that claimed she was embalmed here, during the time that Nathaniel Reynolds' funeral business had been operated from one of the adjacent buildings. Billy also mentioned the visit from the two ladies who also said they had seen the ghost of a young girl standing on the landing headed toward the second floor; whatever the case, the tales of a young girl's visitations among guests who stayed here had become quite prolific. And yet Annie Lee Reynolds, daughter of Colonel Daniel whose pictures throughout the house closely resemble the girl so many say they've seen, lived to be eighty-two. If it is indeed her ghost that people claim to have seen here, why exactly has she continued to manifest as the youthful visage of her former self, while still an energetic young girl? Could the ghostly images of a child seen at Reynolds Mansion not be the same spirit Robinette said she contacted? Could there even be more than one child whose spirit may continue to linger here?

The Hope Diamond and its peculiar mystique also arose during the course of our conversation, and while I began with discussion of the more interesting physical properties the stone is known to bear—specifically it's tendency to emit a pinkish ultraviolet glow under certain conditions—Billy made certain to remind us of the supernatural qualities also associated with what, by all intents, could easily be referred to as a haunted stone.

"You know, you have to mention the curse, if you're going to mention the Hope Diamond," Billy joked with me.

"Well go ahead, I'll let you do that for us," I offered instead.

"It was rumored to have had a curse," Billy began, "although Evalyn Walsh McLean always said she just allowed the good and the bad to battle themselves out around her neck. But the McLean family did have a lot of sadness, and it was believed that the diamond had brought much of it. Even Young Mamie Reynolds didn't want the diamond because of its past, and so Senator Robert Reynolds (her father) sold it to Harry Winston, the famous jeweler. And Harry Winston didn't even keep it... he donated it to the Smithsonian in Washington."

"Where it resides today," I interjected.

"Even the courier that delivered the Hope Diamond to the Smithsonian was injured in an accident after dropping it off," Billy told us, adding a final chill to this already strange story of the diamond and the numerous dangerous affairs associated with it.

"I had no idea," I said, amazed. "Wow."

"It just has such a past to it," Billy continued. "They believe it may have been cursed because it was stolen. It was originally called 'The French Blue,' but after it was stolen, it was cut down to the size it is now. So I think that has a lot to do with the reason people say it has a curse."

"You know, I've heard an earlier legend," I said. "The story was that there was an Indian god—or rather, some statue that represented this god—which some explorer had come across. He found the diamond there, embedded in the eye of this character." Indeed, there is a legend that surmises a connection with India, which had been the only known producer of diamonds going as far back as the seventeenth century. After all, it was there, around the year 1642, that French traveler and cultural anthropologist Jean Baptiste Tavernier, known for his pioneering trade with India, would first discover a large, 118-carat blue diamond while visiting South Asia. According to Joseph McClean, great-grandson of Evalyn Walsh McLean and an authority on the diamond's history, the legend of the jewel's origins makes the bold claim that the stone was, in fact, "stolen from the eye of an idol worshipped by the followers of a Hindu god," perhaps one of the Avatars of the supreme god Vishnu. "As a result of this alleged act," McLean wrote in 2011, "the story is told that the angered god, as a means of enacting vengeance, placed a curse on the robber and all of the diamond's subsequent owners."

Tavernier would go on to sell the diamond, then referred to as the French Blue, which in all likelihood went to King Louis XIV of France in 1699 for a hefty sum of 220,000 livres, packaged along with a patent of nobility issued by the king's Finance Minister. It would pass hands with time, coming into the possession of Marie Antoinette, and would later be stolen (or stolen again, depending on one's belief in the earlier story of its origins) in 1792, remaining missing until at least 1812, when stories of a large blue diamond in the possession of a merchant named Daniel Eliason began to surface in England. The passing of two centuries—and more than the worth of several lifetimes—would come and go before scientific investigation finally confirmed in 2008 that the Hope Diamond that emerged in England around 1830 was, without a doubt, cut from the same stone Tavernier retrieved from India in the seventeenth century.

"Even if some of it's not true, I have to say this: the legend of the diamond contributes to the mystique that's been kept," I continued. "Even the actress from the early twentieth century, May Yohe, talked about how she thought the diamond brought her tremendous bad luck. So everyone talked about this, and of course, the young Evalyn Washington McLean, wife of the Senator, committed suicide while she was the present owner of the diamond, at age twenty-five.

"Tragic story," I added, concealing somewhat my own deep remorse for the circumstances surrounding young Evalyn's death. "And she, of course, was the young beauty whose picture now hangs in the parlor here at Reynolds Mansion." I couldn't help but glance out into the hallway as I spoke, my gaze wandering with unrewarded hope toward the parlor, where I could imagine the curves of Evie's dress falling around her slim and graceful figure as she lounged there, cross-legged, on one of the room's cushioned canapés. How many times had she visited here, I wondered, while married to the Senator? What kinds of thoughts might she have kept to herself, hidden away from the world behind those brown eyes; thoughts which escaped slowly amongst the spirits that accumulated at this place... each and every time she had entered that very room?

❖　❖　❖

The remainder of the evening's broadcast went along smoothly, though we never managed to hear any of the "spirit voices" we hoped would reveal themselves through Chris's microphone. His audio array had been of specific interest since, while the other three microphones in use had been powered condensers, Chris was using a specially designed *dynamic microphone* built for broadcasting, which operates through a process of electromagnetic induction. For years, many parapsychologists have noted the peculiar consistency that microphones of this variety seem to have with regard to recording what is called *electronic voice phenomenon* or EVP, where strange, presumably bodiless voices appear from nowhere, and yet manage to appear on audio recordings (at times interacting with live operators in the environment). One fascinating example of this had occurred at a haunted house in Ireland, where paranormal investigator Mark Cowden, had been recording audio of a spirit medium remotely from another room. As the medium had been asking questions, Mark was monitoring audio being recorded in the room, when suddenly a faint, yet discernable voice began *responding* to the medium's dialogue. Mark was able to relay the answers issued by this disembodied voice back to his medium partner, using radios each member of his investigative team had been carrying. Furthering the incredible nature of this experience, this remarkable set of circumstances had also occurred in the presence of a BBC film crew, who had been rolling tape while the bizarre events unfolded.

Cowden related this remarkable experience in a book, which he gave the appropriate title of *Spirit Voices: The First Live Conversation Between Worlds.* Additionally, Mark joined us on the Gralien Report, live via Ireland, for our September 11, 2011 broadcast commemorating the Terrorist Attacks on the World Trade Center in 2001. We managed to discuss his groundbreaking research regarding EVP, even despite the fact that his expecting

85

wife was due to go into labor at almost any moment. It was an evening to remember, to say the least.

And such had been the case with our evening here at Reynolds Mansion, just as well, with or without the accompaniment of any spirit voices. By the end of the second hour, Billy retired from his place behind our guest microphone in order to prep for an early morning that was already mere hours away. Matt, Chris and I gathered our equipment together hastily once we had finished, and within a few minutes we had broken down the majority of our broadcasting equipment and returned it to the carrying cases piled in the corner of the library.

"I think I'll be heading out," Matt told us, having just returned from a phone call with a lady friend. "Trinity wants to meet downtown someplace. Were you guys planning on going anywhere?" After all, it was somewhat customary, especially during warmer weather, for the three of us to drive into town for a nightcap following the live show.

"Well, it looks like there may have been a change of plans," Chris said, fiddling with his headphones.

"Yes, since Billy reserved the mansion for us this evening, and there are no guests here, Chris and I may stick around a while and take photos," I added. In fact, just prior to the broadcast, Billy had taken us by guest room Claudette on the second floor; one of my favorites for both the décor, and a particularly vivid painting of a Cajun woman hanging above the smaller of the two beds in the room. Should we decide to stay the remainder of the evening, he had offered us the room for the night.

We saw Matt out on his way to the front porch, and stood outside chatting for a few minutes while he and Chris smoked cigarettes. There had been a mild break in the storm for the few minutes we spent outside, but a strong mountain breeze still whipped against the pine trees that danced high above the back lot. I was the first to return indoors, while Chris remained outside with Matt finishing his cigarette, and passing the staircase, I changed course at the last moment, following a strange impulse and entering the parlor across from my intended destination. It appeared as though this room and the study adjacent to it had begun a veritable war of flowers, competing against one another mightily in an effort to win fondness and affection from me. A confessed bibliophile, I admit to the strong appeal any room will have on my psyche if the walls should appear lined with books; in the case of Billy's library, a distinct majority of these were odd or old volumes, some dealing with historical figures relevant to the mansion itself, while others touched on such things as vampirism, hauntings, and the eldritch or unseen. Despite the obvious intrigue such a collection will have in the eyes of a devoted seeker of strangeness such as myself, the parlor boasts a unique charm of its own, and one of equal magnitude to its rival across the foyer. Here, rather than the summation of knowledge committed to worn and discolored pages from elderly books, emotion comes bursting from the many paintings lining the walls; a large portrait of Fred and Helen Faber, the previous owners of Reynolds Mansion prior to Billy's acquisition of the property, hangs above the fireplace, in addition to sepia renderings of family members related to owners both past and present. Small, framed photographs adorn the end tables, commemorating jolly times of yesteryear, along with an authentic memo written by Senator Reynolds encased in glass beneath his portrait on the wall. And of course, there is Evie's lovely portrait above the bar; stopping only to catch the Christmassy aroma off a large bowl of dried potpourri along the way, I headed in her direction, and removing a glass from the bar, I poured a modest amount of apple brandy into my vessel before taking a seat on the couch nearest the fireplace. Chris's footsteps could soon be heard as he reentered the building, and coming down the hallway he joined me in the parlor.

"So what does the night have in store for us?" He asked.

"How about a glass of brandy, for starters." Chris obliged, taking my cue and heading over to the bar.

"Good thing you've armed yourself with plenty of film," I said. "Whether or not any ghosts decide to show up at this late hour, I think tonight, with the entire place to ourselves, will offer a fine opportunity for you to pursue your photographic habit." Chris, having embraced his inner bohemian, had adopted a penchant for analog photography several months beforehand, using a variety of film types and speeds in an impressive array of vintage and new cameras to document our various investigations and inquiries into the unexplained. From a scientific viewpoint, some would even argue that, for reasons similar to our preference in using dynamic microphones for recording EVP, photosensitive chemical properties of film that involve electromagnetic processes of capturing light may be more effective for use in spirit photography.

And yet, to any untrained eye, we nonetheless might have been mistaken for a pair of red-eyed hipsters, keeping odd sleepless hours and partaking in healthy amounts of the house liquor stock.

We moved our operation to the dining room, once we had armed ourselves with notebooks, cameras, and a small voice recorder. It was approximately eleven-thirty in the evening, and despite having paid the mansion many daytime visits, this was only the second time I had managed to stay in the building well after hours. Chris and I tiptoed through the downstairs, careful not to make any loud, obvious noises that might wake our host, who had retired to his suite on the third floor.

"Too bad you don't still have that TriField meter," Chris lamented, referring to a quality EM detector a friend had retrieved after lending it to me for similar previous investigations.

"Well, I'm not too concerned about the loss right now, honestly." Indeed, rather than catering to the so-called "science" of prime-time ghost hunting, tonight I was more focused on observing the environment; any subtle changes, odd noises or sensations we might feel, or especially, any sounds or images that might be rendered during the experience.

Rounding the large dining room table, I moved past Billy's portrait of the pretty and dark-eyed Felicity from Chretien Plantation, and positioned myself alongside the dining room windows that looked out toward the garden. Chris had been standing over by the server ahead of me, doctoring another cup of hot tea with vitamin supplements, when I first thought I heard a noise from the kitchen area—identical to the noise I recalled during my first night alone at Reynolds Mansion.

"Did you hear that?" I barely had time to ask before I was looking toward the kitchen door. Chris, having obviously heard the same noise, was standing there peering through the dark glass into the pantry. At first, I thought the shape beyond the glass had merely been a peculiar reflection; then it suddenly became apparent that the silhouette I watched was *moving*.

"Oh God," Chris managed to choke out.

The dark shadow of a man had moved so quickly from the back of the kitchen that neither of us had been given time to process what was happening; he burst into the room toward Chris, the hinges squeaking on the door as it swung open.

"Did I scare you?" He exclaimed.

It was Billy, who had entered the building through a back door toward the side of the kitchen.

'Hell yes you did!" Chris said as Billy laughed.

"I thought you'd retired for the evening Billy?" I asked. "Five o'clock comes awful early."

"Yeah, I'm headed that way now. I had to run out to the truck for a minute while I let the doggies out, so I just came in the back door."

We laughed as we finished our conversation with the clever trickster, convinced that his scare had been intentional, and bid him goodnight once he finally started his way toward the stairs. The little parade of bulldogs waddled along excitedly after him, and Scarlett paused on the landing only long enough to peer at me through the railings for an instant. As quickly as they had appeared, her little red eyes were gone again, relegated to the light stomping of stubby legs as they made their way to the third floor.

Once the air had settled again, Chris and I began our vigil, moving slowly from room to dimly lit room, with only the occasional flash of Chris's cameras illuminating our surroundings. We spent close to an hour on the first floor, and then heading up the stairs, I slipped out of my shoes, leaving them on the staircase landing, and continued up the stairs silently while Chris and I split up, entering the guest rooms of the second floor and spending time in each, noting our surroundings and any sensations we gathered from the environment. After another period of observation, we returned again to the first floor, knowing that any visit to the upper levels of Reynolds Mansion at this hour might result in a chorus of barking, and recovering my loud, leather-bottomed brogues again, we returned to the library.

"What now?" Chris asked, collapsing onto the couch, noticeably more tired than I was.

"We wait," I said, removing one of Billy's editions on Hollywood monsters from a nearby bookcase. "I still have hopes that one of our ghostly residents might make an appearance."

I slid onto the leather couch facing the doorway, and began thumbing through the pages of the book I had retrieved, feeling almost that if we simply acted like we stayed here all the time, some apparitional presence might come sauntering in and join us. I realized my idealism all the while, accepting the odds against any likelihood that a ghost might appear for us, even given these unconventional circumstances. Nonetheless, I believed that if a ghost should arrive at all, here might be as good a place as any— and better, in fact, than some—for it to happen.

My study of ghosts and vampires continued from the vantage of the couch, glancing up frequently in case some strange form should appear in the doorway. Before long, my associate, whose recovery from the holiday sickness making its rounds had taken a toll on his energy level, was dosing on the adjacent couch. I continued on for another half hour or so, but still there were no visitors to come along, entering tonight's chamber of nevermore dreams, and fulfilling my eerie desire to hold conference with the deceased members of this household.

Chris finally sat up, stirring a bit. "Mmm," he croaked, coming out of his sleep. "Anything happening yet?"

"No such luck," I said, still gazing toward the foyer. Chris got up and stretched, rubbing his nose and yawning.

"Well I wonder if I should head up towards Claudette's room now, or if we should begin carrying things toward the car?" Indeed, it seemed that whatever it was that was happening at Reynolds Mansion this evening, it didn't care much about involving wayward spirits or other strange happenings… at least as far as my company and I were concerned.

"Yeah, let's start loading out. Place seems a little too calm tonight, anyway."

We gathered the last of our belongings, and made a first trip out to the car, filling the back seat with boxes of microphones and other equipment. On our way back in, Chris stopped on the staircase, pulling the box of Marlboros from his shirt pocket.

"I'll be right behind you," he said, lighting his cigarette.

I went on inside, and again found myself stopping outside the parlor on my way to gather the last of my belongings. Evalyn's warm expression, now unlit, still seemed to glow from the far end of the room.

"So nobody cared to join us tonight," I said aloud, as though conversing with the slim and snowy visage on the wall. I caught myself; almost feeling like the sentiments I had expressed had been rude somehow.

"That's alright," I said, correcting my attitude with a smile. "There will be other nights to come." I left the room, and returning to the porch again, was surprised to find Chris standing close to the door this time, rather than over by his usual spot near the ashtray beneath the awning of the adjacent building.

"Everything okay out here?" I asked.

"Yeah," Chris said, though he seemed a bit shaken. "There were two dogs out here a moment ago, that's all."

"Dogs?" I said, a bit alarmed. "Scarlett and Rhett didn't get out, did they?"

"No, these were much larger dogs. They were dark colored, and they were fighting like hell, right over there in the garden."

"Fighting? Well where did they come from?"

"I have no idea," Chris said, putting out the butt of his cigarette on the sole of his shoe. "They just appeared out of nowhere, while I was standing there smoking. They were really getting into it, and kinda caught me off guard, so I got up here on the porch to get out of their way." By now there were no dogs visible any longer, though faintly in the distance, I could still to hear their occasional yelping and growling. I stepped out into the hint of moonlight that had worked its way through the clouds overhead, and the angry cries of the dogs, intermingling with the wind whipping the pines nearby, caused a mild shudder to emerge around my shoulders.

"Come on," Chris said, gesturing from the doorway. "Let's get the rest of this stuff and hit the road." We entered the mansion again together, and I walked from room to room, turning out lights in various places no longer in use. On my way out, I nodded one final goodbye to Evie.

"Goodnight," I said. "I'll see you again."

Chris and I rejoined outside the dining room, and as we carried the last of our belongings with us out the door, we caught the latch, making certain nobody could enter again until sometime tomorrow. The rain had resumed by now, which had begun to moisten the hair on our heads as we walked toward the end of the driveway. Then, just as we left the garden, I stopped and turned around, looking back at the old house, which remained alone like some vague apparition against the glowing clouds of the still hours.

"I do wonder sometimes what the hell it's all about," I said under my breath. As we left the property, Reynolds Mansion stood taciturn and empty behind us, as though taunting us with its silence. And somewhere off in the distance, those damned dogs could still be heard barking, uplifting their woeful bellowing like unearthly hallows to some cold and wicked master of the night.

"What hounds are these, that hunt the night?"
The shepherds asked in fear :
"Look, there are calkins clinking bright;
They must be coming here."

The calkins clinkered to a spark
The hunter called the pack;
The sheep-dogs' fells all bristled stark
And all their lips went back.

"Lord God," the shepherds said, "They come,
And see what hounds he has;
All dripping bluish fire and dumb,
And nosing to the grass.

"And trotting scatheless through the gorse,
And bristling in the fell:
Lord, it is death upon the horse,
And they're the hounds of hell!"

JOHN MASEFIELD, "THE HOUNDS OF HELL", 1920

WANDERLUST

"I've got all I want on this mountain and all I can do. I don't entertain. The happiest job in he world I've got— making sure (Mamie) grows in happiness, equipped for judgment and stability and a good life."

ROBERT REYNOLDS, CHARLOTTE OBSERVER, JULY 10, 1955

WHILE THE RENOVATIONS NATHANIEL AUGUSTUS REYNOLDS would undertake at Reynolds mansion following the turn of the last century were brought about with attention and care, the same cannot necessarily be said of his relationship to Mamie's youngest son, Robert Rice Reynolds. Though Nathaniel worked to fill the void of fatherhood left in the lives of his brother's children, it is understood that the young Bob Reynolds would develop a personal distaste for his uncle-turned-stepfather, and left much of his parental influence to that of mother Mamie and other female family figures. Perhaps it was the sense of seclusion that stemmed from this relationship that led to Robert's loner tendencies; by an early age, the youngest Reynolds boy had already developed a fierce self-reliance, and stood almost unequaled among his peers. These characteristics would eventually provide the gumption that would fuel the world travels and general wanderlust that would follow, as well as the political career that would manifest in later years. Thus, in the long lineage of colorful and hopeful characters that have variously graced the halls of Reynolds Mansion over the decades, we return again in our narrative to those eras long past, when times were simpler, though often no less troubling.

Young Robert Reynolds was described by biographer Julian M. Pleasants as "bright-eyed and tough as a hickory nut," having allegedly been leader of a street gang in his teenage years that the *Asheville Citizen* referred to in 1932 as being "feared and admired throughout Asheville." In 1898, not quite yet the age of fourteen, Bob hopped a train for Charleston, South Carolina, where he would board ship and work as a dishwasher on his way to Jacksonville, Florida. Continuing southward, he rambled about parts of Florida for quick work and easy meals before taking a job as a cabin boy on a fruit boat bound for Key West. Eventually, Reynolds tired of the drifter lifestyle, and after nearly being caught stowing away on a train back in Jacksonville, wrote home requesting that Mamie wire him money for his return trip. Years later, in his 1913 book *Wanderlust,* Reynolds would summarize the adventure thusly:

> I returned, wiser of course, and somewhat disappointed, truth to tell, in not having captured a ruffian. However, I was glad enough to have saved my skin.

Reynolds returned home, and eventually pursued his education, attending Weaver College and then transferring enrollment to The University of North Carolina at Chapel Hill. Among his superlatives while there, the 1906 UNC yearbook listed Reynolds as a member of the German Club, Secretary and Treasurer of the Geological Club, President of the Buncombe County Club, Athletic Editor, and a host of other titles. "Gaze upon the manly features of a globe trotter," the caption read by his image, "a foot ballist and a newspaper man in one. For four long years he pursued his ambition—an N. C. sweater, and when he got it he hugged it to his bosom and departed from our midst. He was born with a prosperity for yarn spinning, and this proclivity he carefully cultivated until it is second to none."

And healthy amounts of yarn spinning certainly would emanate from the youngest Reynolds over the years; in addition to becoming the editor of *Asheville Magazine* in 1906, he would travel to Washington D.C. later that year and serve as a clerk at the *Washington Times.* After a brief stint out west that followed, Reynolds returned to his alma mater to study law, and though no record of ever having attended classes after enrollment exists, Reynolds

A youthful Robert Reynolds at his desk

was nonetheless admitted to the North Carolina bar in 1907, only after trying his hand at amateur boxing over the summer during a visit to California.

Having opened a law practice with his brother in 1908—and despite his potential lack of any formal training in this area—Reynolds' return to Asheville soon resulted in his introduction to Fannie Menge Jackson, the daughter of a wealthy judge from New Orleans with holdings in the coal field industry. Thus, though short, their marriage was happy and fruitful; Fannie passed away, however, only five years later after being stricken with pneumonia, leaving a sum of two hundred thousand dollars to her widowed husband and their two children, Frances and Robert Rice Jr. This would be the first of many wives, and many losses, that Reynolds would sustain in his lifetime.

Robert was not one to remain single for long, however, and would go on to marry is second wife, Mary Bland, one year after Fannie's passing. Bland, of Augusta Georgia, was only seventeen at the time she married Robert; no doubt, the wedded life, along with the pressures of helping raise his two children, did little to foster happiness between them with such a difference between their ages. The two divorced soon afterward, following claims that Mary had been mistreating Robert's children. Then in 1920, while visiting New York in a customized Ford pickup with a camper built onto the chassis, Reynolds accidentally struck an attractive French-Canadian model named Denise D'Arcy as she crossed the street. Though barely harmed at all, Reynolds courted the twenty-three-year-old beauty during her "recovery" (though some variations of the tale say he had visited her for reasons that more likely involved insurance following the incident). Regardless, the two would soon be wedded, though the marriage only lasted two years, due primarily to the culture shock Denise sustained from moving to a mountain town like Asheville.

The fourth wife of Robert Reynolds was a former Zigfield Follies girl named Eva Grady, better known by her stage name, Eva *Brady*. The two met while Reynolds was still married to Denise D'Arcy, though following his divorce to the latter, Grady and Reynolds would eventually wed. Renowned for both her physical attractiveness and her sharp intellect, she had seemed to relish in the life shared with a man who had begun his rise into political life and public notoriety. Poor health had been one of Grady's initial reasons for visiting Asheville early on, having invested in the widespread belief in its healing mountain air. Grady would eventually die from complications with a brain tumor at the youthful age of thirty; she was the second of Reynolds' five spouses that would meet an untimely demise, though as time would show, yet another was destined to befall the folds of heartache that enveloped the Senator's love life.

Robert's experience in world travels, having already visited Europe once before he attended college, would greatly broaden his view of the world and social issues at hand. Even as a young man, Robert was remarkably cultured and well-traveled, and it is said that throughout his years abroad his friends would often receive post cards from such locales as Calcutta, Hong Kong, or Berlin, as detailed in both of his memoirs, *Wanderlust* and *Gypsy Trails*. These, in addition to the pursuit of his many varied interests and practice in criminal law, eventually coalesced to spur his involvement in the community and issues of the day, and thus, like many of his ancestors, Robert eventually decided to enter politics as well, sporting his undistinguished air as a tool in helping earn the trust of potential voters. Having been skilled not only in wandering about, but also the occasional pandering of homemade snake oil to raise money for train tickets, Bob's skill as a talker and a showman proved more than beneficial once he announced a bid for the North Carolina Senate in 1932. Of course, the senate hopeful had manage to gain experience in other more practical areas, too; he had lost to J. Elmer Long in the Democratic primary in an attempt to secure the position of Lieutenant Governor in 1924, followed by an unsuccessful senate run two years later. The 1932 election, however, would prove to be as colorful as it was memorable, with Reynolds becoming known for dressing down and relinquishing himself to servitude as his own chauffer in a Ford Model T Roadster convertible, while asserting that his opponent, the incumbent senator Cameron Morrison, was being carried around Washington in a Rolls Royce by a professional uniformed driver. A stark populist streak had emerged early on, though "Our Bob," as he became known to his supporters, was never really pegged as a populist, per se, nor a progressive. He did, however, manage to create an effective persona as a "man of the people." During a speaking engagement, he once battered his opponent's culinary tastes by insinuating that they betrayed a communist streak. "Cam likes fish eggs," Reynolds quipped, "and Red Russian fish eggs that cost a dollar fifty for a little dab. Don't you all want a Senator who's satisfied with just good old North Carolina hen's eggs, that cost twenty-six cents a dozen?" On another occasion, Reynolds even posed in Asheville before the flashing bulbs of newspaper cameramen to receive a "token of luck" from the Buncombe County police chief. The curiously framed (if not staged) photograph included a caption, which read,

Robert R. Reynolds of Asheville, a candidate for
the Democratic nomination for United States senator, is

shown receiving from Chief Monteith of the Buncombe county rural police a rabbit's foot. Mr. Reynolds announced that he will carry the rabbit's foot on his tour of North Carolina in quest of votes and predicted that it will bring him a continuation of what has been referred to as "Reynolds luck."

Indeed, the "Reynolds luck" had been cemented, it seemed; at very least in the minds of the public, given such a bountiful endorsement. And thus, Reynolds, the personable and down to earth country lawyer from Asheville, managed to defeat his incumbent opponent by an astounding margin: he received 65.4 percent of the vote in the Democratic runoff, which was recorded as the largest majority in any North Carolina Democratic primary. Both the *Charlotte News* and the *Asheville Citizen* ran the statement that Reynolds' win over Cameron Morrison stood "probably without parallel for sensation in the political life of North Carolina."

Just as colorful and varied as his interests, Reynolds' political career would be marked with unconventional views and attitudes. To again quote Reynolds' biographer Julian Pleasants, Reynolds was largely a "demagogic isolationist":

> He lashed out at alien criminals and increased immigration while voting against American membership in the World Court. He was the only southerner to vote against Lend Lease. Meanwhile, Reynolds began his congressional career by voting for almost all New Deal legislation and was a loyal supporter of Roosevelt until 1938. He sought reform of American society and improvement in the daily life of the average American

and thought government could provide for the economic and social welfare of the masses with programs such as Social Security and the Wagner Act. Reynolds saw the inequity in society and understood the frustration and alienation of the have-nots.

Paired with his penchant for championing the beleaguered underdogs of Depression-era America, Reynolds would also become known for his anti-Communist ideals and defense of state sovereignty. However, the Senator would just as readily draw criticism, especially later on, fueling controversy with what were often perceived as Nazi apologetics. Reynolds often expressed views in defense of the German aggression in Europe that precipitated World War II. And as an isolationist, though cooperative with the Roosevelt administration, his position as chairman of the Senate Committee on Military Affairs had also served in promoting the controversy that surrounded Reynolds.

An undated photo of Reynolds & staff in Washington, courtesy of Billy Sanders

Reynolds would build a number of associations with political dissidents and controversial public figures, the likes of Gerald L. K. Smith, who published a magazine called *The Cross and the Flag* largely renowned for its propagandist denouncement of the American war effort. The two would also go on to collaborate on a publication known as *The Defender,* as noted by researcher Charles Higham in his book *American Swastika;* this newspaper often featured anti-Semitism and portrayal of Jews as the anti-Christ. Reynolds would also go on to make associations with the likes of controversial Roman Catholic priest Father Charles Coughlin, who during his radio addresses would often bespeak anti-Semitism and the ideas of Adolph Hitler, among others. Due to such associations, Reynolds would at times be painted as a Nazi supporter, and his failing public image in this regard contributed strongly to his eventual political decline.

The political controversy and other events leading up to the Second World War would prove to be pivotal for Reynolds in other ways too, since by the time he had left for his seven-week honeymoon with his fifth wife, Hope Diamond heiress Evalyn Washington McLean, America had already begun to sustain attacks from its German aggressors. These resulted in the sinking the American destroyers *Kearny* and *Reuben James* in the autumn of 1941, and despite his strong feelings toward the issue of American neutrality in the growing global conflict, Reynolds' absence during the debate that followed these attacks showed, for the most part, a lack of enthusiasm on part of the Senator, in terms of performing his duties as an elected official in times of crisis. At the time, and despite the international conflict that had been brewing around the United States' entry into the war, his attention had been focused elsewhere.

And rightly so, perhaps, even if no real justification can suffice other than the romantic precedents involved. His marriages up until this point had already exposed Reynolds as a lover of the company of women, and though described often as a "ladies man," it would not be fair to have labeled him a roué or Casanova. If anything, Reynolds seemed to place much emphasis on family life, and his involvement with the comings and goings of women in his day may have had as much to do with the interests of his children and their upbringing. And yet, by the time he married for the fifth time at age fifty-seven, twenty-year-old Evalyn McLean—precocious and worldly though she was—had herself only barely qualified among the ranks of adulthood. Having enjoyed a long association with the wealthy and famous McLean family during his years in Washington, it was with Mother McLean's blessing and encouragement that Reynolds would go on to marry the young heiress.

Christened Emily Beale McLean, Evalyn the younger would adopt not only her mother's first name (she was the daughter of wealthy socialite Evalyn Walsh McLean), but also that of the nation's capital in the formation of her regal new title. Summarized in a profile that fell just short of endearing, the youngest McLean was featured in *The Pittsburgh Press* on September 14, 1941, which described her as "amazingly precocious," but always driven to boredom by the happenings of the wealthy and famous in Washington:

> What Evalyn Washington McLean is like at 20, few people know.
> She is amazingly precocious. Quiet, bored most of the time, she talks easily with people three times her

age; has been to school only a few months, yet knows more than she could have learned in books.

Since her babyhood she has associated with the great and the near-great of the Capital. Her mother has long been a celebrity collector, and Little Evalyn is completely at ease with G-Man J. Edgar Hoover, the British Ambassador, a Cabinet member or a Congressman.

Or even a Senator, as would soon become obvious. Though the difference in ages between the two may have seemed strange for some, Little Evalyn—painted as something of an old soul herself—had always displayed a penchant for keeping company well beyond her years; the famous Broadway photographer Herold "Hal" Phyfe, only eight years shy of being able to match Reynolds' age, had courted young Evie in previous months, and at the apparent chagrin of the eldest Evalyn. While Phyfe was spurned around the hallowed halls of Friendship, the family's famous home in Washington, Senator Reynolds had been welcomed as a regular guest to Sunday night dinners at the McLean household since his arrival in the capital. To those who knew the family well, it was no surprise when it was announced that the two would be married; Evie, on the other hand, was quoted by reporters who pried for details on the engagement that, "I don't know how it happened—it just happened."

Perhaps no one was more surprised, however, than Reynolds himself, who allegedly had been shocked upon learning that his hand had been offered in marriage to young Evie. Reynolds' aide Hubert Rand claimed in hindsight that the Senator contacted Evie's mother after learning of the announcement, who not only confided to him that she wanted Robert to help see after

Evie's fortune for her, but that her daughter's fondness for his colorful stories and authentic southern charm had grown into genuine admiration and, most important of all, love. "I think I am a very lucky man," he later said of the circumstances.

A seven-week honeymoon in Cuba with Evie would follow, and upon their return to the States, Reynolds came home to find that a revision of his previous attitudes toward the mounting conflict overseas would almost become mandatory. Following the bombing attack on Pearl Harbor, Reynolds gravely misspoke of the circumstances, alleging that Britain had been working to try and drag the United States into the conflict. Newspapers decried Reynolds' assertions, and soon it became evident that his stances toward isolationism, paired along with the earlier pro-Nazi allegations, would now make his hope for a future in politics less than promising. Turning about-face, Reynolds modified his stance on the war effort, expressing unending support for the effort now that the United States had been drawn in. His various publishing mediums reflected these sentiments strongly as well, though the mainstream media clearly viewed Buncombe Bob's sudden support for the cause as merely the politics of self interest, rather than a genuine concern for national affairs. Adding further fuel to the fire, still more allegations of Nazi ties were leveled against Reynolds late in 1942. At this point in the game, there were times where nothing, it seemed, could ever sway the media, let alone the public, from holding such positions against him.

One redeeming moment did arrive in October of that year, however; the arrival of a new infant daughter, Mamie Spears Reynolds, into the family. Despite the joy that centered on the latest incarnation of his family life with Evalyn and Mamie, Reynolds continued to draw criticism for his various political views, activities, and associations. Reynolds' publication the *American Vindicator* had been renamed the *National Record* back during the war, but continued pressures and criticisms would eventually succeed in bringing the periodical effectively to the ground by late in 1945. And prior to this, of course, December of the previous year had marked the end of Reynolds' eleven-year career as a Senator. Granted, the purpose at present is not to examine the political ups and downs of "Buncombe Bob's" career in Washington, as far better examinations have been afforded us elsewhere in this regard (see *Buncombe Bob: The Life and Times of Robert Rice Reynolds* by Julian M. Pleasants, University of North Carolina Press, 2000). In truth, Reynolds would yet return to his beloved Asheville, and settle again on the old mountain that bore his namesake; this final destination would not be attained, however, before tragedy would strike the Reynolds family yet again.

Following his departure from public office, another vacation getaway was planned, during which Robert and Evie retreated again to their southern getaways in Florida, Cuba, and the Caribbean. After several months traveling together, the two eventually came back to Washington, and had been living in an apartment while Robert considered his career alternatives. He was already well enough into his years, but Robert, effectively a jack-of-all-trades by virtue only of his apparent lack of focus, began getting restless again, feeling it would be the antithesis of any southern gentleman to merely exist on the fortune his wife had inherited. Thus, during this period Bob's wanderlust again seemed to manifest, this time in a variety of half-hearted attempts at reentering the practice of law, as well as the purchase of a large farm near Waldorf, Maryland, with the apparent intention of farming timber on the property to sell as pulpwood. This endeavor, like others from around the same time, never really came into fruition.

By September of 1946, Robert and Evie had returned to Friendship, where the two had been staying with Mother Evalyn as she recovered from a broken kneecap. After having lunch with Evie on the afternoon of September 20, Robert left for the timber farm in Waldorf, and Evie retired to her bedroom for what was believed to be a short afternoon nap. The procedure had become routine by now, although she specifically requested on this occasion that she remain undisturbed until Robert returned from the trip to Maryland. Then, locked within the bedroom, Evie medicated herself with sleeping pills in what proved to be a lethal overdose; within two hours, Mrs. McLean had become concerned when she received no answer from her daughter using the house's intercom system, and prompted the family doctor, along with the butler on duty, to break down the door and gain access to the sleeping girl's room. Evie was discovered lying unconscious on the bed, clasping her husband's picture against her breast. An hour was spent in fervent attempt at trying to revive the unresponsive girl, but all measures aimed at saving the young beauty proved useless. Evalyn Washington McLean was pronounced dead shortly after 4 PM that afternoon, at which time her mother made the heartbreaking call to Robert, prompting his return back to Washington.

The heartbreaking romance of the story surrounding Evie's death makes it easy to idealize the circumstances; the mysterious beauty commits suicide for reasons unknown, while holding her beloved husband's image against her heart as her spirit makes its passage from this world. In an effort to be honest, we can rightly assume that Robert and Evie's relationship wasn't a storybook marriage in all its aspects. We can also acknowledge that Evie was known to have suffered mental distress in the past, in addition to an apparent addiction to the barbiturates that ultimately helped claim her life. In the absence of any suicide note, some have expressed great difficulty accepting that the death had actually been a suicide. But there had been other overdoses prior to the one that brought the final chapter of lovely Evalyn's life to a close. On every occasion, she had been discovered in enough time to be saved; but in this instance, with the door to her bedroom securely locked, time had not ruled in favor of her would-be rescuers.

And yes, the locked door, along with the picture of Robert clutched against her breast, paired with the numerous past attempts at overdoses, make it almost impossible to rule out a suicide. Many would assert that the infamous Hope Diamond and its curse had claimed yet another victim; indeed, it seemed that a number of those who came across it were afflicted with ill fortune, or even death. Of course, rumors and hearsay would persist about the family's infamous jewel, lending to speculation about the real existence of some curse that must have caused Evalyn's depression and ultimate demise. But regardless of the circumstances underlying her motives, those close to Robert and Evie said that despite the differences in their age, the two had shared a happy marriage, and that the tragic young beauty who died that day, with the likeness of Robert Reynolds held close to heart, had truly loved the man.

Oh lady love of yesteryear,
Wearing Hope above her breast
Sad, yet striking, with your gaze
That yet stands out among the rest

What perils hid within your heart
What thin young frame didst fall at last?
Was it languish o'er your own regrets
Or from your noble thane's long past?

The years have wandered on without you,
Sons and daughters raised, and going
And you, forever young lost beauty
Left us guessing, of love unknowing

Robert Reynolds would never remarry, though following Evie's passing, he and four-year-old Mamie returned to Asheville to reside in a lodge home near the summit of Reynolds Mountain. Having only returned and settled back in the Reynolds family home place, it was less than a year after his wife's passing that word came from Washington that Evie's mother, Evalyn Walsh McLean, had been stricken with pneumonia. Robert rushed to her bedside, knowing full well that she had never recovered emotionally from the loss of her daughter, and on April 26, 1947, the elegant "Queen of Diamonds" passed away at age sixty. In her will, the use of her home in Washington and its furnishings were left to Reynolds, in appreciation for his service and friendship to the McLean family, and any income made from investments after sale of the home would be granted to Reynolds. McLean's will also noted that Friendship, as well as the collection of family jewels that contained the infamous Hope Diamond, could be sold to ensure the proper security for Reynolds' daughter Mamie.

Despite the heartbreak associated with the loss of both Evie and Mrs. McLean, Robert managed to find an outlet for his wanderlust again with young Mamie, wisely using the fortune they had inherited to take the budding youth with him on educational trips to various parts of the world. While it is known that Mamie had circled the globe at least four times before her thirteenth birthday, it was later said her globe trotting exploits would take her around the world a total of "seven times in lieu of long years in boarding schools," according to one feature in the April 20, 1968 edition of *The Telegraph*.

As Mamie approached her teenage years, she had begun to develop a keen interest in drag racing. By age nineteen, she became the youngest ever car owner according to current standing NASCAR records, employing driver Fred Lorenzen, who managed to win her fourth start on September 13, 1962. Around this time, Mamie had been introduced to Luigi Chinetti Jr., son of the famous Italian-born racecar driver, through her interest in racing, and after several months, it was announced that the two were to be married on Saturday July 27, 1963. Their marriage would not last, however, and just two years later on September 14, 1965, Mamie divorced

Chinetti, only to remarry the same day to a dapper and gentlemanly Kentucky dog handler named Joseph Gregory, whom she had met years earlier at a dog show in Asheville. After marrying, the two made their residence at a beautiful and elegantly decorated home known as the Old Shelby County Mansion in Simpsonville, Kentucky, where Joseph encouraged a thrifty lifestyle for his new bride; he and Mamie had agreed that she would be allotted an allowance of five dollars each day, so as to better assist her in managing her inheritance. The two lived happily together, moving between the Kentucky home and other residential locales they had secured, throughout the south, along with Ziggy, their prize Brussels Griffon.

"The decorator wouldn't let me put my 400 dog trophies out," Mamie told *The Telegraph* in 1968 of her antebellum Kentucky home. "She called them 'cheap silver.' I never told her about Joe's 200 trophies in the garage. Had to hide the dog books, too. As soon as she left, I tossed out the fashionable magazines she had placed on all the tables. I mean, who reads them? Not our dog crowd. We're not much on entertaining."

Nor had Mamie's father been much the entertaining type in his final years, for that matter. On July 10, 1955, the *Charlotte Observer* quoted Reynolds saying, "I've got all I want on this mountain and all I can do. I don't entertain. The happiest job in the world I've got—making sure [Mamie] grows in happiness, equipped for judgment and stability and a good life." Reynolds would remain at the lodge on Reynolds Mountain until February 13, 1963 when—exactly five months to the day of Mamie's first NASCAR win—he finally died from complications from bladder cancer, for which he had recently undergone an operation. Despite the official cause of his fast decline, a fading Reynolds had asked that the press be told instead that he had "died of a heart attack."

Thus ended the life of the colorful southern politician, who despite the rambling interests and worldly passions he had longed for in his lifetime, had lived out his final years in devotion to little

The Senator (top left) and Mamie (center) at her eighteenth birthday party

Mamie, right up to the lavish coming out party he held for her at age eighteen, only months before his own death. With all the past trials and heartaches behind him, it seemed there was one woman that remained throughout the journey into the final sunset of his life, and they had managed to stay very happy in each other's company. Buncombe Bob's wandering was finally done.

According to documents from the U.S. Department of the Interior, concerning Reynolds Mansion's inclusion with the National Register of Historic Places, Senator Reynolds likely spent more time at the Mansion later in his life than he did in his formative years:

> It's uncertain how much time Senator Reynolds spent at the Reynolds Mansion during his youth. His family's principal residence was on Woodfin Street in Asheville but it is very likely that the family visited their country house and perhaps lived there from time to time on a temporary basis. It is certain that Reynolds returned to the old home place frequently as an adult during the years that the house was owned and occupied by his mother and uncle.

Robert's mother, along with her second husband, uncle Nat August Reynolds, had moved permanently into the home sometime between 1929 and 1930, where they resided together for the next decade until Mother Mamie's death in July of 1929. Nat Reynolds retired from the funeral business shortly afterward, and lived there at the mansion until he passed away in March of 1950. Following Nat's death, Robert Reynolds' half sister, the widowed Adelene Hall, came into possession of the old Reynolds Mansion. She and her daughter, Ann Lee, remained there throughout Robert's final years at his residence further up the mountain, until the house was finally sold in 1973 to a Mr. Patrick W. Arabia, along with four acres of land. The house would then pass in 1974 from Arabia's ownership to that of Ralph and Sally Gates, providers of quality handmade brooms. Mr. Gates had been a retired NASA engineer from the Apollo years, who owned a small shop on Wall Street in Asheville. During their tenure at Reynolds Mansion, the lower portions of the building actually served as base of operations not only for their broom business, but also domicile to the flock of Bohemians the Gates had employed for their operation.

A severely overgrown Reynolds Mansion, following years of neglect

For the next three years, the residence would remain occupied only in Spartan fashion, allowing functionality for the broom operation, while upkeep of the historic Reynolds family home had fallen almost completely to the wayside. Severe rainwater damage had begun to compromise parts of the upper structure, while portions of the once elegant porches that lined the building's exterior had collapsed entirely. By the time Ralph and Sally Gates had elected to sell the property, it had already been recommended by city officials that the old building, which barely remained as a shell of its former state, simply be demolished. Sprawling clusters of vines had suffused the exterior walls of Reynolds Mansion, and in many instances, penetrated the sturdy brickwork and crept into the darkened interior of the mansion's sunless walls. Portions of the original wooden floors had been scraped and splintered, and mold had darkened the once ornate trimmings that lined the ceilings of each room. Large and empty, the mansion stood silent and alone on the hill—darkened by day, and noiseless by night—save only for the faded whispers of its ghosts, who begged that the crumbling halls and musty rooms that once carried their voices throughout the place be spared.

How unlikely, it seemed, that anyone would care enough to put the necessary grit behind restoration of an empty old dwelling the likes of Reynolds Mansion; and yet, to the surprise of many, in August of 1977 that's precisely what happened.

Highland Happenings

Candid Classified

BY NANCY BROWER

From the February 21st, 1977 Asheville Citizen Times, *Afternoon Edition*

Can buyers be found for a house candidly described in a classified ad as a "slightly haunted 1847 brick monstrosity?" Sally Gates said the phone rings constantly as callers ask for directions to the three-story, 13-bedroom home she and her husband, Ralph, have named Toad Hall.

Toad Hall, whose name was inspired by the children's classic, "The Wind in the Willows," is on a four-acre knoll overlooking North Merrimon Avenue.

The Gateses are selling the house with its 6,000 square feet of living space because, said Sally, "We need less house and more land."

Ralph Gates was leading software systems engineer on the Apollo lunar module. When the Apollo Project ended, Gates opted for a new lifestyle and learned the craft of handtying brooms. He operates the Double Eagle crafts shop on Wall Street and supplies brooms to other crafts shops in the East. Broommaking apprentices are housed in Toad Hall, which has seen as many as 21 people in residence and 27 at the dinner table, including the Gateses and their four children. "We don't have as many people with us now," Sally said, "and we don't need all this room."

Kitchen Probably Annexed

The kitchen probably was separate from the house in the beginning, Sally pointed out, as she began the conducted tour—one of several each day. "There is supposed to be a wine cellar, but we have never been able to find it. And we have looked in all the places where they might have hidden the family silver from the Yankees. We removed that likely-looking panel under the stairwell and found two batteries for crank telephones."

In a sunny corner bedroom that is not at all sinister, the lady of the house said this is where she first heard "things that go bump in the night."

"See that door," she said, pointing to a door standing ajar. "It won't stay closed. There is nothing wrong with the locking mechanism, no way to get to it from the other side. (They have upended a pool table against it.) But it won't stay closed. I can close it firmly and it will latch. I can come back in a few minutes and it will be open."

She continued, "It was on Halloween night that we first heard the strange crash that seemed to come from this room. I'd heard things before, but I just put them down to old-house noises. But Halloween night, we heard such a noise in this room that we ran downstairs—our bedroom is directly over this one—to see what had fallen. We heard the noise four times that night and never found any explanation for it."

Wide Staircase

Leading the way to the second floor, Sally mentioned that the stairway probably was built wide to accommodate hoop skirts. Curiously, the only items found in the attic, other than some bedrails, were three extra newel posts for the staircase. "Why would anyone ever need even one extra newel post?" asked the tour guide.

A trapdoor at the top of the second flight of stairs closes off the third floor, added to the house under a mansard roof in the 1920s.

It is from the third floor that some of the strange noises come. What noises? "Oh, sounds like people walking around and I know there's nobody up there because the trap door is closed."

Sally dismisses the ghost. "Whatever it is, it doesn't seem to mind us being here. It's not the least bit scary."

The third floor is full of curiosities including a bathroom with a toilet whose water tank is made of oak and lined in copper. The Gateses have refinished the old water closet and call this bath "The Oak Sitting Room."

Porches on three sides once took advantage of the view. They are crumbling. "Don't go out there," said the hostess. "That's a hard hat area."

The swimming pool is empty now, but is fed by a direct overflow line from the old Woodfin reservoir on Reynolds Mountain. The water is cold, Sally said, but free.

Four big dogs escort Mrs. Gates to a potting shed, now "The Grass Menagerie," occupants of which are why the family needs more land. A cow has been sold, but two saddle horses, a pony, donkey, two cats and three chickens remain.

Rundown as its exterior is, the old house has a certain air about it. "I'm told," said Salley Gates, "that years ago, a white Stutz Bearcat was parked out front in the summers. And the yard is just full of lilacs."

STANDING STRAIGHT AND TALL

"Dreamer of dreams, born out of my due time,
Why should I strive to set the crooked straight?"

JAMES MARSTON, "THE EARTHLY PARADISE," 1868-70

REYNOLDS MANSION SAW WHAT, ARGUABLY, BECAME ITS MOST severe and unfortunate period in the years after it passed from the hands of the Reynolds family in the early 1970s. Ralph Gates, who had worked as a systems software engineer for NASA during the Apollo missions, retired from the computing field to pursue making handmade brooms at the place, founding the Friendswood Brooms Company there in 1972. Gates, it is said, managed to learn the specifics of the broom trade from an old mountain craftsman named Lee "Pop" Ogle several years beforehand, while he still worked with the space program. It was Ogle that taught him a handful of unique Appalachian broom making techniques dating back to the late eighteenth century. By the time he had settled in

Asheville, Gates and his story had become an item of certain intrigue, garnering attention from *The National Enquirer*, which at the time was still known for printing occasional truisms. "My new life is centered around human values," they quoted Gates saying, "rather than materialistic values." And yet, perhaps it was Gates and his focus on the human side of things that contributed so heavily to the deterioration of Reynolds Mansion during this period; arguably, a bit of materialism around this time might have done the place some good.

Fred and Helen Faber, previous owners of The Old Reynolds Mansion

While hardly "materialists" by nature, Minnesota natives Fred and Helen Faber were nonetheless of a mind and disposition to greatly improve the place once it came into their possession. "We wanted to do something together," Helen told me during a conversation we had over the phone in June of 2012. "Fred had worked for a corporation for years, and had traveled a lot. Our son was finally through high school, and so we decided we were going to try and do something *together*. We had visited his great aunt over in Germany, who had owned a guesthouse over there. It was a great big old house, and we thought, 'that would be a nice idea.' And I always wanted to move to the south, because I liked the greenery and the warmer weather. So we started looking to see if we could find a big house somewhere, and we contacted a nationwide realtor that sent us a flyer; Reynolds Mansion was on it. And so we drove down and bought it!"

Fred and Helen Faber secured Reynolds Mansion in 1977, but it would be several more years before they actually took residence there. "We didn't move down until January of 1981. We had lived southwest of Minneapolis for four years, and then we lived north of Saint Paul for another seven before deciding to leave for North Carolina. Fred and I had taken a couple more years up in Minnesota, so that he could finish things with the corporation. We let the former owners, Ralph and Sally Gates, stay for a while longer, rather than having it stay empty, because it was in such a state of disrepair. We wouldn't dare leave it empty, but nobody would have wanted to rent it, because it was looking *really bad.*

"Each summer before we moved to Asheville, we would go down for our vacation, and during those visits we would do things like work on repairing the porches, and the sorts of things that we thought really could have been terrible dealing with by the time we could actually move down there. And then, in 1981, we finally did move. When we arrived with our big U-Haul, the Gates were still living there, although they were actually supposed to have moved out by then. So we kept the U-Haul truck for two more days, just to help them move out!"

❖   ❖   ❖

By the fall of 1982, Fred and Helen were not only living at Reynolds Mansion, but had managed to open two guest rooms situated on the second floor, in addition to one bathroom. "The chamber of commerce was looking for rooms for the fall season, so we went ahead and opened, but with a lot of doors that were still closed! And then, during the winter, we closed down again, and by the next year I think we had about six rooms done. Every winter we'd just open a few more like that, so it was a work in progress. But back then, you didn't have to be spit and polished to be open. The guests enjoyed seeing what was getting done as we worked, and it just kept getting better and better. So it was probably at least seven or eight years before we had everything in the house that we wanted done.

"The building had almost been demolished a number of times over the years," Helen recalled. "The Preservation Society had just been formed about the time we were going to buy the place, and they were trying to push through to get it listed on the National Register of Historic Places, because they thought it would save it, since it was in such disrepair. After our restoration work, the Preservation Society awarded us its annual Griffin Award.

"The porches were one major part of the restoration," Helen said. "One side had sunken down about twenty inches, because they had set the floor of the porch right on top of the brick wall there. Then, of course, as it rotted, the porch just kept settling down more and more, and so that was a major area. It took us well over a year to get those rebuilt. The entire side to the right of the front door as you go out had fallen down. And of course we had to put all new wiring in, as well as all new piping for water.

"Fred, with the help of our son, took the old boiler apart, and managed to haul the entire thing up those steps and out of the basement somehow. It was a coal fire boiler, and so we put a new boiler in at that point, and I think it was in 1979 that we had an oil fire boiler installed. I had to have it replaced again just before I sold the house, too," Helen said. "Those coal fire boilers were really large!"

"The building was rented out as a sanitarium, back in the days when they used to send people to the mountains that had tuberculosis. I know that one of the stipulations for Dr. Elizabeth Smith when she obtained the house for use during that time was that the chimneys be extended, so they could have heat provided to the upper floors. So the coal fire boiler was probably installed in the 1920s, or some time around then.

"None of the original furniture was still in the house by the time we acquired it from Ralph and Sally Gates. The furniture we used was all hauled down from Minnesota. I got a lot of things from a lady who had lived in a great big Victorian house in Illinois. She would downsize occasionally, and call and ask if I wanted to buy this or that. We bought a lot from her, and we'd go to flea markets, and anything eBay was throwing out we'd take."

Despite the numerous restorations that took place over the years, the majority of the building's interior remains largely unchanged. The large dining room had once served as two rooms, until Nat Augustus Reynolds took out the separating wall between them during his renovations. And adjacent to the dining area, some of the most significant updates that would modernize the home would be the Fabers' redesign of the kitchen during their stay. "While a lot has changed about the building since Fred and I had it, the biggest changes have been to the outside grounds," Helen admits. "It was completely wooded early on. You couldn't see the house from the street at all. When we first bought it, the lane was different, too. You came up off of Merrimon Avenue about where you would go into the shopping center there, and then it came through the trees, and curved around, and came up to the front of the house, and then went by where the cottage is now.

"The man who owned the property all around us wanted us off of that driveway, because he wanted to do something with that property down below. He had put a stipulation when he had bought it from Anne Lee Hall that he could move the driveway any time. And so he moved us over to the side, because he had to give us a way to get up to our land; he couldn't leave us land-locked! So then the driveway came up from behind, and came around the south side, around the house and out behind the cottage. Years later, when Billy and Michael were interested in it, the developer's attorneys contacted me, to see if I would change the driveway, and come in off of Senator Reynolds Boulevard. At one time, I had to maintain that other driveway, and the developer was just being nasty, as far as putting big trucks up our driveway and everything. And I had asked to come in off of Senator Reynolds Boulevard already, but he wanted to buy the house, probably to tear it down. And he said no, that it would make my property more valuable that way, so he wouldn't do it. So then when I got ready to sell

Reynolds Mansion, I figured I wouldn't do anything about it, and that if Billy and Michael wanted to change it that was fine.

"For a time, Fred and I lived right there in the house, in the master bedroom there on the first floor. Our son and daughter in law came down at one point to stay with us, because they had thought for a time that they might want to run a bed and breakfast, but after staying with us, they decided that wasn't for them! So they left and went back to West Virginia. We had made the downstairs of the adjacent cottage into a little apartment for them, and so then after they left, Fred and I decided that we'd move into the cottage. It would give us a little more privacy, and room for more staff. But up until that point, we had always lived right there in the main house."

Much like the present owners, Helen Faber and her husband had been fascinated with the building's past, as well as the stories of those who had lived in it. "I was very interested in gathering history about the building when I lived there, and often times the Reynolds family relatives would stop through, because they had heard somebody was working on the place. They would give us all kinds of stories or tidbits about it. We never did find any really old pictures of the house or anything from back before the porches were added, when it was just a two story colonial house. We had several Reynolds family reunions there—three of them, I think—and they were all relatives attending, but still nobody ever came up with early pictures of the mansion."

❖ ❖ ❖

Despite the absence of photos of Reynolds Mansion in its early years, there have been times throughout the decades, as most who visit it will quickly learn, that colors from the building's past have still managed filter through, perhaps in spectral form. "I guess I'm a realist, because I don't believe in ghosts," Helen told me with a laugh. "The whole time that Fred and I lived in the house, we always had cats. I always thought that cats would certainly be able to feel something if it were there, but they would sleep on any bed they could get to!" Despite her own lack of unusual encounters, to say that Helen hadn't shown some interest in the stories of ghosts at Reynolds Mansion would be inaccurate. During our conversation, Helen shared a number of stories she had heard about her antebellum home over the years, and though having never personally seen or felt anything during her time there, she had nonetheless been made privy on many occasions to the stories of others who claimed they had.

"We had guests that were absolutely sure that there were ghosts at Reynolds Mansion," Helen explained. "In fact, there was at least one guest that would come back every year because of it. He started out in the room on the third floor, at the top of stairs on the left, which is now called 'Maggie's Room.' After he stayed in that room, he was just *sure* there was something in there. And then he moved over to what is now Billy and Michael's suite across the hall; there, this man said he *did* actually see the apparition of a lady. He later picked her out of one of the pictures I had hanging downstairs, showing the four girls and the mother that had lived there in the house, and the one he picked that matched the ghost he saw was Annie Lee Reynolds.

"Then we had a little girl who used to house sit for us, and her name was also Annie. At one point, she looked at that same

130

picture our ghost hunter had, and said to me, "who is that lady?" I told her it was Annie Lee she had pointed out, and she said, "She was looking out the third floor window when I first drove up to this house!"

According to Helen, Annie Lee's ghost appeared this way to most who saw her, just as she looked in the family picture hanging on the Mansion's first floor. In the photograph, all the Reynolds women had posed together: mother Susan Adelia Baird Reynolds, along with the four surviving daughters, Mary Sophronia, Susan Evelyn, Julia Matilda, and of course, Annie Lee.

"I think it was taken around 1886. I had that picture hanging in one of the front parlors, but I don't know exactly where in the house it's hanging now. In the picture, Annie Lee had dark hair, and looks quite severe. But back then, of course, in pictures everybody looked severe. She never married, and lived there at the house her entire life." The fact that Annie Lee Reynolds never married remains slightly mysterious; having lived at Reynolds Mansion throughout her life and up until her death on Independence Day in 1948, it seems strange that she would remain a bacheloress well into her later years. Despite the wealth of data that does exist about the Reynolds family, little else is known about Annie Lee Reynolds, and having passed away more than half a century ago, few who might have known her well in their adult life may still be living that could shed any light on her personality and habits. Had there been some reason she shunned the courtship of would-be suitors? From the looks of pictures that still exist from Annie's youth, she was by no means an unattractive girl. Could there have been some physical ailment, or perhaps another condition that might have caused her to become reclusive? These were interesting questions, but no answers seem to exist in the immediate sense.

"The one gentleman I mentioned," Helen continued, "the fellow who always would stay there looking for ghosts—he really delved deeply into this stuff. He would tell Fred and I that he kept getting the feeling something terrible had happened at the mansion, like a murder or something. But I never heard anything like that! None of the former residents died mysteriously, but I know that Billy and Michael have said that the particular room at the top of the stairs on the left, Maggie's Room, is where they've found stuff has been moved, and things like that."

Indeed, Maggie's Room did have a certain atmosphere about it, and following my first night alone at Reynolds Mansion, at which time the room had served as my quarters for the evening, I recalled being afflicted with an odd restlessness. I had seen no ghosts, nor any phantoms moving chairs or luggage around, but there had certainly been the sense of there being company of some variety; had it been Annie Lee Reynolds visiting in the night? Or perhaps, had my imagination longed badly enough to have such an experience that my subconscious willed itself into sleeplessness in the excitement of anticipation? Furthermore, could it have been that others who visiting as guests in the past, some of them aware of the legends about ghosts haunting the place, had done the same? Or were these presences that so many have said they felt over the years the lasting impressions of past members of the Reynolds family, who not only lived there throughout their lives on earth, but perhaps continue to reside there in the afterlife? One might ponder how such ghosts would feel toward the numerous changes the house had undergone over the years. Would someone like Annie Lee Reynolds have shared the enthusiasm for renovations, additions, and restorations that the owners of more recent decades have shown?

"We were the third bed and breakfast that opened in the area," Helen told me as our conversation began to wind down. "Now, of course, there's probably about fifty of them. And so, we did stay really busy for probably the first ten years, and then we got more independent. We wanted more time off, and so we kind of slowed down as more inns opened up in town, and we didn't really market ourselves as much, like Billy and Michael have done. They really wanted to get up there and be first, and have done things right. But for Fred and me, I guess that really wasn't our goal.

"Fred passed away on June 24, 2003. I continued running the business up until the October of 2008, and after that, I just didn't run it as a bed and breakfast anymore, although I continued to live there until I sold the house to Billy and Michael in 2009. Like myself, I know Billy has collected a lot of material about the house, and has been in touch with a lot of people, and so he's probably collected a lot more than I had. And of course, I left everything I had found that pertained to the house with Billy when I moved, also."

Before we closed, I felt an urge to ask Helen to share one of her fondest memories from her time spent at Reynolds Mansion. I noticed during our conversation that Mrs. Faber has a very ebullient variety of laughter, and though she paused a moment before responding, that characteristic chuckle soon initiated a bright, quick stream of memories about the restoration process she and her late husband had undertaken.

"I just loved seeing it come back," she said, "returning to looking beautiful again, standing straight and tall. It was really rough when we bought it, and later after we hosted the family reunions there a few times, many of the family members were very upset after I announced my plans to sell it. They wanted to know how I could do that, and so while they were there for that last reunion, I showed them a slide presentation we had done for the Preservation Society, and none of them, except one who was from Florida, had been familiar with the way the house looked before we bought it. And so, when I showed them what it looked like, they could not believe that it had ever gotten to such a bad state. They just always knew that there was a house there, but none of them had seen it at it's worst.

"I was kind of upset when I returned and found that all the trees were gone," she admitted. "We used to love to be isolated there. As you came around the corner, it was like, 'oh my gosh, you can't even see it from anyplace else, and it's here!' We liked that isolation. It probably wasn't good for business, though, and Billy and Michael wanted to have it more visible. They planted so many trees, of course, to replace the ones that had been removed. But you couldn't even see it the way the landscape looked before, and we always felt like this little surprise as you came around the corner. And so that was very hard for me to get used to, and also because you approach the house completely different from how you did before. The first time I took my granddaughters up there, who of course love to swim in that pool, they said as we drove up, 'they moved the house.' Of course, that wasn't the case, so when we went around back, then they tried to argue that it was the swimming pool that had been moved! You can get a bit disoriented seeing it so completely different than you remember seeing it before."

The changes, however, really seem to matter little to Helen Faber, who still loves seeing the mansion whenever she can, and enjoys dropping in for visits at her former residence. "It's nice because I know Billy and Michael so well that I feel like I could stop in and see them any time. They have done a terrific job. I'm so thrilled that they found me, and that I found them, and I couldn't have turned it over to anyone better than them."

With little doubt, if the old walls of Reynolds Mansion could speak aloud, we probably would find that the sentiments shared regarding its present owners were very similar.

Dear Micah,

It has been a busy morning, but I have jotted down a few notes in relation to my husband and my involvement with The Reynolds Mansion. If these thoughts are helpful in any way, I am glad to share.

In July of 2009, my nephew, Michael Griffith, e-mailed and asked that, for a good time, I call him for a "proposition." Since his work had taken him far away from the mountains of Western North Carolina for a number of years, I was totally unprepared to hear that he and Billy were considering fulfilling a long time dream of purchasing and opening a Bed and Breakfast in the Asheville area.

Since I operated a small local Real Estate business, I jumped at the opportunity to do some initial legwork to see what might be available in the area. Working in secrecy, with only my husband Don in on this "covert" operation, I worked with Michael and Billy long distance to research and visit various properties that they had an interest in. Don was in Alaska at the time, and when I first mentioned that I had visited "The Old Reynolds Mansion", he immediately became excited. Having grown up in the Asheville area, he was very familiar with the rich history of the house and its association with the Hope Diamond. His prophetic statement was "That's the property they want". He has never been more right on.

My initial visit to the Mansion was a drive-by, and my first reaction was surprise that this stately mansion had escaped my notice for all of the years that I had lived in Asheville. The grounds were terribly overgrown, but the potential was obvious. My first report was to Billy, and he recalls the term "massive" when I described the main house to him. I relayed that the afternoon sun was streaming into one of the second floor bedrooms, making it feel so warm and inviting despite the size. A wonderful surprise, after the purchase was complete and renovations were underway, was the honor of having my name attached to that exact room.

Under the "too co-incidental to be a co-incidence" tab was the Bob Reynolds letter. My husband was an estate dealer in the mid eighties. He and a partner had purchased the estate of the widow of the former editor of the Asheville Citizen Times, George McCoy, who was a close friend of the Thomas Wolfe family. There were actually letters from Thomas Wolfe found in this estate, which are now housed at the University of North Carolina. Many other interesting artifacts and letters became part of our private collection, which through several moves had been boxed away for a number of years. Sometime after Michael and Billy re-opened Reynolds, Don and I were looking through these stored documents and came across a letter addressed to Col. Charles Lindbergh. On closer inspection, Don realized that the letter was from the office of Senator Robert Reynolds, and was actually signed by the Senator. This fact had initially eluded us, before the name held its current significance. Of course Don gave the letter to Michael and Billy, and they currently have it on display with their growing collection of historical documents related to the Reynolds family and the Mansion.

Fortunately for all of us, the purchase of Reynolds Mansion coincided with our recent downsizing, and the need to place a number of antiques and collectibles... both family-related and those that Don had acquired during his estate business years. We were happy to see these personal treasures find such a beautiful and fitting home. One of the current sets of Reynolds china was our grandmother's, which I had been in possession of since her passing in the nineties. "Mamma Ruth" loved to entertain and was past district president of "The Home Demonstration Club" and of her local "Garden Club". She would have been honored beyond words to have her portrait hanging in such a historically significant mansion, and to know that visitors from all over the world were enjoying breakfast on her personal china.

All the best,

Claudette Childs

Michael Griffith's Aunt

United States Senate

COMMITTEE ON BANKING AND CURRENCY

March 22, 1934.

Col. Charles A. Lindberg,
New York,
N. Y.

My dear Col. Lindberg:

  This will serve to introduce my friend
Mr. Harry W. Love, who is interestedwith me, as
chariman of the Executive Board of the United States
Flag Association, in some very important preliminary
work in connection with the national War on Crime.

  Any consideration you may show him or any
assistance you may see fit to lend him will be greatly
appreciated.

  With kindest personal regards,

    Cordially yours,

    Robert R. Reynolds

RRR-r.

The authentic 1934 letter from Senator Robert Reynolds to Charles Lindberg

Seven

FAMILY MATTERS

"One need not be a chamber to be haunted,
One need not be a house;
The brain has corridors surpassing
Material place."

EMILY DICKINSON, "ONE NEED NOT BE A CHAMBER," 1891

AS HUMANS, WE OFTEN TEND TO OVERLOOK THE EFFECT WE have on our surroundings. Every random thought, and even our most constrained actions, may go on to affect people and circumstances far greater than just ourselves. To apply this concept on a global scale, it may bring to mind such things as rainforest depletion and urban sprawl, the effects of which become more obvious over time. But how seldom we consider the minutia in our daily existence that can drastically change aspects of our surroundings. Imagine something so insignificant as the smoldering filter of a spent cigarette, falling from the window of a passing motor vehicle; this miniscule burning ember could easily land on a patch of grass just dry enough to ignite a brushfire capable of scorching an entire mountainside.

The same general principles apply themselves to life and living just as well. Throughout the course of our lives, interactions we have with others can have drastic effects on their lives, ranging from the negativity senseless violence brings, to the profundity of random acts of kindness. But arguably, individuals aren't the only things affected by the life and actions of humans. As our earlier example has shown already, a brushfire capable of destroying acres of land, along with the millions of living things that populate such a habitat, can very drastically change the elements that constitute an environment, leaving a very lasting impression on that place, and perhaps forever changing it.

One of the most terrifying experiences I ever recall having that had to do with ghostly phenomenon occurred at the Old City Jail in historic Charleston, South Carolina. The place was in operation from the beginning of the nineteenth century, all the way up until 1939; around the same time many famous movie monsters of the Universal company had begun stalking and, occasionally, stumbling across the silver screen. The jail itself, complete with Romanesque Revival features and a rear octagonal wing added in the 1850s, often more closely resembles a decrepit old castle standing there in the moonlight, as Spanish moss sways from the trees nearby and the salty Charleston air slowly corrodes its ancient foundations, which variously housed murders, serial killers, Confederate prisoners of war and, of course, the famous seafaring pirates of the Atlantic, over its more than a century in use.

There certainly were stories of ghosts seen in the building; in particular that of a former slave who was said to whisper things into the ears of tourists visiting the place from just over their shoulder; some would claim to turn around and catch a glimpse of this man, while others say they would hear deep voices emanating from within the halls of the place. But the thing that stood out in my mind during my own visit there many years ago had more to do with the energy the building had within. Immediately upon entering, what I would describe as a sinking feeling began to occur, setting the tone for the remainder of the night. While the size of the group with me during our visit was modest, the entire building felt very confined, especially in rooms where rust stains from small cages stained the floor, hinting at the kinds of conditions many of the men incarcerated here were kept in. In many of the larger rooms in the building, entire wall faces were decorated with crude graffiti picked and scratched into the stone surfaces of the cells. Some of the writings were beautiful, or even elegant; many were filthy, hate filled inscriptions launching attacks against the men keeping them here, or perhaps the circumstances that led to their incarceration. Still others were filled with obsolete words and expressions, as well as long-forgotten references to things of yesteryear, which bore little meaning at all in today's world, save only the emotion that may have gone into the act of being etched in stone at Charleston's Old City Jail. In this instance, one need not look for any ghosts simply to be able to find evidence of those who came before us here; the very energy of the building itself had been permanently marked with the range of emotions and negativity that this place bore for decade after decade, and no room within the place could escape it.

Fortunately the energies that remain at Reynolds Mansion are pleasant ones, for the most part, the majority of which are merely holdovers from an earlier time, when the family members who came and went from the place went about their daily lives. There have been, on occasion, those who visit the place and remark that there are tremendous feelings of pain, or perhaps neglect... maybe even sadness or death. Arguably, throughout the course of the Reynolds' tenure here, some members of the family must have died in the place; many more would have endured struggles and personal strife as they met the random chances and events life tends to throw at us. And yet, despite the sorts of "negative energies" that a handful of people have claimed to have experienced or felt here, it seems unlikely, based on historic records maintained over the years, that any kind of questionable deaths or other circumstances involving nefarious intent ever transpired.

I had recalled one journalist during the 1960s describing that she found the place incredibly gloomy and strange during her visit, which of course, occurred during the tenure held by Ralph and Sally Gates, at which time the building had arguably seen one of its very worst periods. Today, few would ever walk into the home and say they found the place frightening or gloomy. And yet, the obvious truth here—and one so simple that is can become easily overlooked—is that the environment of any locale will be affected by its layout and décor, as well as those individuals housed within its walls. Even when wandering the grounds of Reynolds Mansion in the still hours of the night, I can hardly profess to ever feeling like the place is dark, depressing, or frightening, though an occasional eeriness does catch one's interest here and there; this is especially the case in the parlor, where Evie and Senator Bob Reynolds' paintings seem to keep watch from their outposts on adjacent walls, monitoring the comings and goings of the place after nightfall.

Indeed, the sensations one feels at Reynolds Mansion are almost entirely good, and few would ever argue that the building's rooms each have their own colorful character to them... a *personality*, almost. After all, each had been named for the lovely matriarchs of Billy and Michael's families, and many of the individual rooms bore the likenesses of these ladies in photos and elegant paintings. Thus, along with my probing study of the home's former residents, I considered whether the families associated with the people here today might also have helped contribute to the "energy" this place now had. To be thorough in my research of the strange happenings going on here, I decided that my study of the modern Reynolds home might benefit from having some knowledge of Billy and Michael's family members just as well. In particular, I wanted to know more about those ladies after whom many of the building's guest rooms had been named; but the big question in my mind had been whether this, in any way, could have contributed to the stories of hauntings occurring here now?

Linda Griffith, a Western North Carolina native, was born in Yancey County to parents William and Katie Wilson, and still resides there today with her husband David. When Linda and David married, the couple moved to Hickory for a short time, but soon returned to live closer to her place of her birth.

Michael, like his mother, was born here in the mountains, and after graduating high school, attended college at Mars Hill in Madison County. He had worked an internship with J.C. Penny, and shortly after graduating he relocated to Nashville, TN, where he first began working for the Enesco Company, providers of gifts and other items designed for celebrations. After this, his business took him to Jacksonville Florida, where he first met Billy. They remained in Billy's home state for a number of years, until their professional aspirations finally led them North to the Windy City of Chicago.

"Michael kept it pretty secret that they were looking for a bed and breakfast in Asheville," Linda remembers. "My sister, Claudette, had been working to help them find a place, but in truth they had been looking at a number of places in different states around the country."

Despite their search for a new home, as well as a new business, Linda told me that one of Michael's primary reasons for wanting to come home had largely to do with family. Linda's parents are still alive today, but when David's mother passed away a few years ago, Michael had felt that he had missed out on time he could have spent with her in her final years.

"I know that Michael had been quite upset that he hadn't gotten to spend more time with his Nannie Vera," after whom another of the rooms in Reynolds Mansion is named, as well as Linda's mother, Katie. "He felt he needed to come closer to home. Both my parents are alive, and David's father is too, but he's now ninety-four-years-old. I think Michael really wanted to be able to look after the family, in a sense."

"When they bought Reynolds Mansion, I was really overwhelmed," Linda admits. "I didn't see the same vision they had for the place. Michael is very business minded, and it's not something I ever thought I would see him doing. I know Billy, on the other hand, has *always* wanted to run a bed and breakfast, so maybe it was just a matter of time. But the two of them do work well together.

Linda's husband, David, has also worked as a carpenter for a number of years, lending his services toward helping Billy and Michael complete many of the revisions and restorations when they were preparing Reynolds Mansion to be reopened as a bed and breakfast. "He did bathrooms, and closets, and took out the wall between two rooms on the third floor that make the suite where Billy and Michael now stay."

"I love it now, and David and I both feel very blessed. We love the fact that we have a place like that to go visit every time we come through Asheville."

I asked Linda about the decision to name one of the rooms after her, to which she explained that all of the women in the family on both sides had been chosen for the various rooms and the names they were given. "You know, I also have a daughter named Cynthia. Once Billy and Michael had opened Reynolds Mansion to the public, she asked her brother why they didn't name one of the suites in the other buildings on the property after her. Michael said, 'it's because to qualify for having a room named after you, you either have to be dead, or *really close*.' We all had a good laugh about that."

"Doesn't sound like you're very close, dear!" I confided to Linda. "You're hardly one of the ghosts I'm looking for… but I'm glad they were able to name a room after you, regardless."

After my conversation with Linda Griffith, in addition to countless evening visits to the mansion spent wandering the house alone in silence, I eventually decided to return again in the afternoon for a more casual visit. Billy and I arranged for a day when he would have several hours in between various interviews he was conducting for hired help, so that I could speak with him about not only the house, its rooms, and what supposedly went on in them between past, present, night and day, but also the stories of the people whose portraits now adorned those walls.

The master bedroom of Daniel Reynolds, once a key fixture of the home and its builder, is now a quaint room colored in soft blue and greens. Old mahogany headboards and dressers line the walls, and above the fireplace a painting of Lila Hilliard hangs on the wall, after whom the room is named today.

Billy's great grandmother Lila was born about 1903, and having been raised on a farm, life had been very hard growing up, especially living in a rural community in North Florida. "Towns were pretty small back then, and there weren't a lot of people where she lived," Billy told me. "They were from a little town called Bell, Florida, which is in Gilchrist County."

Lila had dark eyes that matched her complexion, was remembered for being very upbeat, and loved to laugh. "She had a very infectious laugh," Billy said. "She loved everybody, and

Great Grandmother Lila Hilliard

never met a stranger; that's what people always said about her." There were, however, two things in life that Lila would never do: she would never visit a movie theatre, nor would she ever wear bathing suits. According to the recollections of family members, it is said Lila would always profess that she, "wouldn't want to be doing either if the Lord come back!"

Lila eventually married a hard-working man named Clarence Hilliard, and had four children by him. Their names were Inez, Ernest, Mevalee, and Clarence Lila Hilliard, who had been given both his mother and father's first names. Clarence and Lila ended up living with Clarence's parents after they married, who according to Billy, bore from the lineage of the Eastern Cherokee Indians.

The relationship between Lila and Clarence had been far from perfect. Billy admitted as he gazed up at Lila's portrait on the wall how he always felt that Lila had been a victim of mental abuse, as well as infidelity while married to Clarence. "I've been told that he spoke unkindly to her, and often didn't treat her all that well. But when you hear that kind of thing, you have to also take into consideration the time during which they lived, and the sorts of hard lives they had. I think their whole existence—the marriages, and everything in their lives—were hard back then."

At some point, Clarence's infidelity led to contraction of a sexually transmitted disease, which was, of course, passed along to Lila also. Keeping the condition a secret from his wife, Clarence had sought treatment for this independently and was cured; hence, he never bothered telling Lila what had occurred. Lila, on the other hand, began to fall ill. "She got to where she could hardly even talk, and just couldn't function," Billy said, referencing photos resting on the bedside table nearby that featured a noticeably weakened, and barely recognizable Lila Hilliard. "Lila stayed in a room in the back of the house, and had to be fed through a funnel for a long time. But at some point, she was finally sent to the Chattahoochee Mental Institution, which despite the name, was really more of a hospital or osteopathic sanitarium." Lila was eventually cured of her illness, and in a story remembered by her daughter Inez, when the family went to retrieve Lila from the hospital, she had been wearing a red velvet coat. "Inez saw her mother standing at the top of a flight of stairs in that coat, looking strong and healthy again. She said she was the most beautiful thing they'd ever seen."

Lila returned home, and despite the troubled marriage, she stayed with Clarence for the remainder of her life. The two would eventually go into business together, managing a grocery store, as well as a tavern called The Melody Club, which lasted for several years. Their youngest son, Clarence, had decided to build the grocery store, although he had also been a very talented dancer and pianist, which had prompted the addition of The Melody Club onto the same building. By night, musical entertainment would abound on one end of the building, and come morning, each day Lila would be next door, serving breakfast in the kitchen area of the grocery store. Around this time, Lila's daughter Inez met J.D. Osteen, whom she married on a ceremony planned for Mother's Day. Thus, Lila always would refer to her son-in-law as "her Mother's Day present." As one might expect, every seven years the same holiday would of course fall on Inez and J.D.'s anniversary, and Billy to this day always remembers the Mother's Day as being "a special time in our family." I wondered, standing here and talking with him about all this, whether the significance of that particular holiday could also have influenced the present decoration that adorned not only this particular chamber, but virtually all of the mansion's guest bedrooms throughout the house.

Lila died of a heart attack at age fifty-nine. When paramedics arrived at their home following her death, they found her husband Clarence knelt over her, clutching Lila in his arms. Despite the tumultuous nature of their relationship over the years, he had seemed to refuse to let go of his wife when the heart attack occurred, and as paramedics began their attempt to retrieve Lila from a hysterical Clarence, it took several of them to finally loosen the grasp of his strong arms. Lila was buried shortly afterward in a beautiful blue nightgown, and Billy's mother, Glenda Corsaro, remembered seeing the characteristic sweet smiling expression on Lila's face at the funeral. "At the funeral she wore a very soft, blue nightgown," Glenda later told me. "She was absolutely stunning, even in her death." As many widowed partners will tend to do, in the weeks that followed Lila's death the grief-stricken Clarence would begin to develop a number of health problems, including high blood pressure, for which he eventually sought treatment. In his later years, Clarence always would say that Lila had been the nicest and truest person he had ever known, and that despite the hard life they had lived, he never recalled ever hearing her complain about their conditions. For Lila, the light that illuminated happiness she would find in life came from within.

My meeting with Billy's mother, Glenda Corsaro, took place shortly after my initial conversation with Billy about Lila and the rest of the family. When we met, it had been only a few hours prior to her departure for Florida, where along with her husband Michael, she resides today. After our introductions, Michael and the others left Glenda and I together in the library, as I pulled out my MacBook and began recording our conversation.

Glenda Corsaro and the author in the library at Reynolds Mansion

"You know," Glenda said as we began, "and I mean this in a very good way—but when they told me there was an author coming to visit today, somehow I had pictured you being older."

"Oh yeah?" I responded. "I get that a lot, you know."

"Well they didn't tell me I was gonna be talking with some handsome young gentleman!"

152

I chuckled, and thanked her for the compliment. There was hardly any ice left to break at this point, and we went right into our discussion about her mother, Inez Hilliard Osteen.

Much like her mother Lila, Inez had lived a very hard life. Working around the home, she had acquired the reputation for being an excellent country cook, using an intuitive sense of how to prepare things, rather than relying solely on recipes. But despite her attributes, Inez was typically very quiet, and often shy. According to family stories passed along over the years, her father Clarence had once even tried to pass off her hand in marriage to a suitor who offered, as an exchange for the agreement, a healthy hog!

Before the man she would ultimately come to love and marry, J. D. Osteen, came along, Inez had been married once before while still in her mid teens to man who had shown frequent abusive tendencies. Inez had been terrified of the man, and when he would get drunk and angry in the evening, often raising his voice, she was known to run outside and hide beneath the house where they lived. During that time, she had become pregnant by her first husband, though the child was born with a cyanotic heart defect, sometimes referred to as being called a "blue baby." The child only lived a few months, and died eventually while being held in his mother's arms. Inez's child was buried in New Hope Cemetery near her home in Gilchrist County.

"That marriage didn't last long," Glenda told me of her mother's first marriage. "Inez eventually ran away, She was just so young, and he scared her to death. She ran away, and never went back to him." With few other options at the time, the desperate young Inez returned home to her mother and father.

At that same time, a young man named James Delton Osteen had been boarding with the Hilliards, and upon her return to the family home, Inez and James, who of course went by the nickname J.D., first became acquainted. Their friendship had amounted to slow labor at first, because Inez, who had been described as "very old fashioned," was also very shy, and still insecure from her previous marriage experience. However, as Inez slowly began to open her heart to J.D., a romance blossomed between them, and the two eventually became engaged. As Billy had told me, the two were married on Mother's Day, prompting Lila to always call her son in law "her Mother's Day present."

J.D. Osteen during World War II

"You couldn't have asked for a better father," Glenda remembers of her father James. "He wasn't a Christian growing up, though he never was really a rowdy person. He just hadn't really accepted the lord at that time, and he did sell beer in the grocery store. After he became a Christian, out went the alcohol!"

The events that brought J.D. to a religious life had been strange, and unfortunately, nearly fatal. While turkey hunting one day, another hunter had mistaken J.D. for being the quarry he sought, and without properly identifying his target, had mistakenly fired on him; the spread of the shotgun peppered J.D.'s lower extremities, badly injuring his leg. The shooter, obviously aware of what he had done by that time, left J.D. lying injured at the scene, and never reported the fallen woodsman he left behind to die.

As is the case with many an injured man, while lying there in the forest wounded, J.D. felt that it was finally an appropriate time to converse with his maker. "He knew he had been shot," his daughter recalled, "and he said that he literally just talked with God, one on one, and acknowledged that maybe this was where he had needed to be for God to get his attention." Uncertain as to whether he would survive at all, J.D. promised that if he could be spared in this instance, and allowed to return to help and live alongside his beloved family, that he would live out the rest of his days in service to the lord. "He did recover, of course, and after that," Glenda said laughing, "you didn't ask if you were going to church on Sunday. He'd say, 'don't ask, just be ready'.

"Once he became a Christian, it was like he was just absorbed with the scriptures. He ended up becoming one of the best Sunday school teachers there was." J.D.'s faith carried over with regard to how he felt toward his intended shooter. J.D. had known the man, who also lived in Gilchrist County, but never contacted or met with him following the accident. At one time, he allowed information to be released through certain channels that had been aimed at convincing his shooter that he had died, to see if the man would come asking about the death; this never occurred, however. Throughout his years, J.D. had many attorneys that offered to represent his case, but he declined. "Daddy was not a suing man," Glenda said, noting that he would always say there was no point in doing something like that. "I'm not a rich man," he had said many times, "and I'm not gonna get rich doing something like that. And furthermore, that man has to wake up every day wondering if I'm alive or if I'm dead. That's hard enough to live with."

J.D. and Inez at the family store, the site of his second brush with death

The hunting accident hadn't been the only time J.D. was subjected to what easily could have been fatal gunfire. During his years running the family grocery, there had also been a failed robbery attempt, during which J.D. sustained four gunshot wounds, and yet miraculously, still managed to survive.

"Daddy was left handed, and always kept a gun under the counter. When he closed, he would also take that gun with him to the car. When dad closed the store up that night, he was getting into the car, and heard someone call his name." His assailants had been armed and hiding, while a young woman with them had been sent into the store several minutes earlier as a scout, to be able to observe that he was preparing to leave. "When he turned around, they shot him from the waist up, four times in the chest."

The doctor that examined him said the way J.D. had been standing had saved him; two bullets striking the center of his chest had apparently ricocheted off his sternum, the other two entering his shoulders and causing minimal damage. J.D., still carrying his weapon, fell to the ground, and yet managed to fire back at his assailants. A single shot fired at one of the shooters, who had been crouching at the time, entered his back near the end of his spine, and lodged in the base of his skull near enough to his brain that removal surgery would have been risky. He too survived, and was sentenced to time in prison for the attempted robbery and murder.

Inez and J.D. remained together the duration of their lives, living in a number of homes together with their children, each built by J.D. himself. In their later years, Inez became quite prolific with her fishing, as the family had settled along the shore of one of their favorite properties, obtained by J.D. through wealth accumulated in the ownership of the three grocery stores he had owned and operated. "She could out fish any man at Santa Fe Lake, just like her daddy," Glenda said, "and she'd catch fish by the tub full. Inez worked with J.D. in his stores for years, and when they finally bought the property by the lake, he had always said, 'I'm gonna build us a nice home out there one day.' And he did. So by the time they moved out there, Inez would stay at home, and that's when she got into the fishing, and then that led to chickens, ducks, geese, and peacocks. She loved them all.

"When it got to looking just like a regular farm out there at the lake, then Inez decided she just had to have a little baby goat. So she went and got one, despite J.D.'s hesitations. That little thing would go everywhere: it would try to get under her dress, and it would want to come inside the house, or it get up on top of the car... and so J.D. finally made her get rid of him. That little goat was a sight."

❖   ❖   ❖

It was there, at the lovely country home on the shores of Santa Fe Lake, where Inez and J.D. spent the remainder of their lives together. For a number of years, they also enjoyed the company of their son, Jerry Osteen, and daughter Glenda, who at age sixteen, came to meet the man she would eventually marry, albeit under rather unusual circumstances.

Inez had been driving along with Glenda in the passenger seat, when a patrol car's siren could be heard behind them. Indeed, it seemed that Inez had accidentally turned the wrong direction down a one-way street, and now the law had intervened, and perhaps fate to some degree, too. The officer that came to the window was Bill Sanders, in his mid twenties at the time. As he had signaled the ladies to bring their car to the side of the road, Sanders had initially assumed this otherwise mundane traffic stop would produce a warning ticket, as many others earlier that week had already done. Walking out into the hot Florida sun, he arrived at the driver's side of the car, and as Inez rolled her window down, she began to converse quietly with the officer, in keeping with her usual modest demeanor. Sanders, on the other hand, quickly became aware of the young teenage beauty in the seat next to her, and decided that a change of plans was now in order.

"Ma'am, do you know you just went down a one way street?" Inez admitted knowledge of her mistake. "Well I'll tell you this," Bill continued, a smile now lifting the corner of his lip. "It may not matter to me, so long as you don't mind me taking your daughter to dinner one night."

Needless to say, there was no citation issued for Inez that day. "He looked at me," Glenda said, "and from that moment on, he never left me alone."

"Did he take you away in the patrol car that day?" I asked with a laugh.

"No, he had to be careful because I was still young!" Glenda replied.

Bill and Glenda did begin seeing each other however, although they had to do so very carefully, for even in those days the difference in their ages may have been looked upon with question, especially for an officer of the law. Glenda soon married Bill, quitting school in her senior year at age eighteen to be with him. But a difficult coupling would begin to emerge as the stress of Bill's demanding profession began to weigh on their relationship. Bill, after all, was a tough man, and his hard, stoic personality— along with the several years' difference in ages between them— made it difficult at times for he and Glenda to relate to one another. Glenda often had great difficulty understanding Bill when he would come in at night like a thunderstorm whipping around, slamming doors and showing no interest in talking about the labors of the day. They soldiered on for close to two years before things finally began to unravel.

"We started having trouble right after we got married. Bill was tough," Glenda described. "It's not easy being married to police officers, or firemen, because they have a big strain on them.

And so, we did not have what you would call a great relationship. He was a wonderful person, and would give you the shirt off his back, but he was kind of hard to live with, because he was a police officer. And you have to be kind of hard to do that kind of work. And me, being totally different from him, we just sort of collided sometimes, like I couldn't understand where he was coming from. Sometimes, he would say, 'well you're just immature.'

William Sanders, arriving from a turkey hunt

And I used to get sick of hearing that; I mean, I may have been young, but I wasn't quite that immature. I had a little bit of sense!

"We were married a total of about twelve years. During those twelve years, we had several separations... about three of them. In one of the separations, he divorced me, which was just out of the blue, because at that time nothing was happening. We were doing really wonderful. He just walked in one evening and said, 'I've worked overtime enough, and I'm going to get a divorce.' It really blew me away. It shocked me so that I just put the spatula down—I was frying pork chops that evening—and I just said, 'okay, I think we need to talk!' He said there was really nothing to talk about, and that he had just made his mind up. I said, 'well if that's the case, then there's no need to finish supper. I'll just pack my bags, and go home!' My name was on nothing, but it crushed me, just *crushed* me. But you would have had to know William to understand it. He was raised very differently from the way I was, just totally different. He went through more than I did coming up, so when I thought about it years later, I overlooked a lot of it, because I know that that was a lot of what the problem was: that we couldn't seem to get together, and also that I *was* young, and that maybe I just wasn't ready for a twenty-six year-old man. You know, he'd been around, and I hadn't.

"Bill became a detective later on, and he was a great detective… one of the best. He had a lot of informants that helped him get information, and there were a lot of write-ups in the paper about him; but I'm just telling you, people who are that involved with their jobs are hard to live with. He had people in accidents that were just mutilated. His own brother was killed in a car wreck, and Bill was the one that cut the clothes off of him. I mean, he went through some things that, really, most people just couldn't handle.

"So when he *did* get time off, he wanted to get away. He'd just go off to the woods and hunt, and leave me with the kids, which wasn't really good for the marriage either. But looking back, I can understand that perfectly clearly now, and we really did become very good friends after the divorce. We weren't exactly what you'd call bosom-buddies, but I could call him any time I needed to, and when my daughter Sherry got married, we were all there together. We had no problem at all after that.

"But you see, after that first divorce, William and I did remarry. Billy was born during our first marriage, and then Sherry came along after we remarried. And after that second divorce, I think he would have done it again. After all those years, I remember one time he called me out of the blue, and just said, 'would you like to go and have dinner, just you and me?' I said *no!* Then he asked if I would want to go to the beach and spend a weekend, but I had to say, 'Bill, no. And it's not that I wouldn't like to go with you, but we've been there, done that, and we don't need to go there anymore.' And he said okay, but I believe he would have remarried again. Even though we stayed friends all that time, we knew we couldn't really get along. But that didn't mean we never cared for each other. And he never married again.

"You don't just stop loving someone," Glenda added.

❖   ❖   ❖

Of course, perhaps no room in the entire mansion had the mystique or strange appeal that Maggie's Room had attained, with its reports of ghostly tomfoolery that would often perturb guests, along with the occasional author who might dare to spend a sleepless night in the company of Annie Lee Reynolds' ghost.

"Glenda," I asked, "can you tell me which side of the family Maggie would have been on?"

"Oh yes, Maggie was my father's mother. She was the one whose husband, Tom Osteen, was killed as a young man in a terrible car accident. He was a nice looking man, but I was only ever shown one picture of him. His death put a very hard time on Maggie, and my uncle Roy, J.D.'s eldest brother, ended up having to quit school to help his mother raise the other kids. I wasn't around Granny Maggie as much as I was Lila. Maggie was not at all in the disposition that Lila was; they really were totally different women altogether. Granny Lila had a hard time growing up, and she was still a lovely person, whereas some people have a hard time coming up, and it stays with them. They're just not happy, and my Granny Maggie seemed to be that way most of her life. I never saw her joyful like Lila was, and I think it's because that hard period in her life just never left her."

"Some people just carry it with them," I interjected, wondering now about the fact that the guest room named after Maggie had also been the one from which so much of the supernatural activity had seemed to emanate. In a psychological sense, the presence of symbolism that might be attached to a location through the attribution of a name alone could have at least some small effect on the physical surroundings. A clear example of this was featured in an experiment I heard of where objects were handed to participants in a study, and told that they belonged to famous celebrities. A pen, for example, which may have belonged to a former American President, would be held and marveled over; on the other hand, a sweater that had supposedly been owned by a serial killer would be shunned and shied away with disgust. The funny truth behind the entire experiment, of course, is that there was never any famous ownership that could honestly be attributed to either object; but through the simple act of misleading people to believe that there had been famous owners of certain repute, people's attitudes toward those items would change as well, and whether or not the attitudes were justified. Granted, most of the people visiting Reynolds Mansion had no knowledge of who Maggie Osteen even was, let alone the kind of troubled life that she had lived. Therefore, it stands to reason that no direct association could be drawn between people's mere perception of strange phenomenon that may be occurring in the room, and the troubled life of an individual who lived more than four hundred miles away in a rural part of Northern Florida. Equally curious, however, is the fact that the most haunted portions of the Reynolds home, at least as remembered in recent times, were the third floor additions that came much later in the building's history. Then again, I hear countless stories of brand new homes that seem to carry with them the staples of an old, haunted house: the thumping and bumping, objects moving by themselves, disembodied voices, and even the occasional appearance of full-bodied apparitions. Sure, maybe some people simply want so badly to have an otherworldly experience that they simply make things up, or perhaps unknowingly *allow themselves* to believe things that simply aren't reality. On the other extreme, it stands to reason that under the right circumstances, certain people may subject themselves and others to varieties of psychic phenomenon that literally would amount to "haunting" themselves.

After our discussion surrounding Glenda, Billy's father, and the other family members on their side of the family, I then decided to ask Glenda to describe her own memories of Billy's childhood. At this point, I had become interested in seeing what events might have led him to wanting to dive headlong into the demanding business of bed and breakfasts, let alone one that was purported to be haunted.

"I was about twenty when I had Billy. Then right around twenty-two, his sister was born. I was pretty scared, because I had lost one child. There would have been another one, but I lost that first child. When Billy came along, I didn't even know I was pregnant with him. I had a kidney infection, and went to the doctor. He said, "You're pregnant!" And I almost went hysterical; I had gone through so much losing that first baby that I wasn't planning on trying to have another one at that time. I had wanted to wait a while! But everything ended up being fine. Billy was a big baby, nine pounds and seven ounces.

"Growing up, Billy was never real tight with his father," Glenda added. "I think that, as he got older, they probably got more in tune with one another. He and I were very close, on the other hand, and I used to love to take him driving with me places." She recalled how, when Billy was just a little child, there was a large brick house that he would always point out to his mother as they drove past it.

"He was maybe just walking, when I would take him riding in a little car seat. There was one road we'd go down that went down by the duck pond, where we would have to go a lot to get to town. There were some very beautiful and elegant two story red brick homes there by the duck pond; that was kind of the "exclusive" area. And let me tell you, every time—and I mean *every* single time I would pass that road, he would always point to this one particular house, and he would say, "Momma, you see that house? One day I'm gonna buy you that house." And after he grew up, I thought about that. Every home he's lived in since he's grown up has been an enormous home. He loves big houses, and he loves to decorate them."

"Makes sense," I admitted. Billy certainly had a fondness, along with a general knack, for decorating and maintaining a large home. "Are there any other stories about his upbringing that come to mind?" I asked. Glenda issued a waggish sort of giggle as I said this. "The kind maybe that he wouldn't tell me, but that you would," I added.

"That I would?" she asked, as I now returned the chuckle to her. "Well one thing is I used to get onto him about reading. He read more as a young boy than anyone. He was fascinated by books."

"Now surely he doesn't like *books*," I said, gesturing at the volumes lining the walls of the library that surrounded the conversation pit where Glenda and I sat chatting. She just smiled, shaking her head.

"You know, I couldn't understand then, because I was busy raising he and Sherry, and keeping myself at home to do those sorts of things. So I wasn't thinking in the terms that he really was getting good things out of those books at the time. To the contrary, I just thought he was *killing time,* which I guess was a mother's way of thinking at that point in his life. But as it turns out, it was probably the best thing that ever happened to him, really.

"Another thing I used to get really upset with him about was frogs."

"Wait, *frogs?*" I repeated.

"Yes, animals he brought into the house. We had snakes, and we had raccoons, and I would open the closet and a frog would jump out. I'd open desk drawers in the room and there would be frogs in there, too. He was just fascinated with animals, and had them everywhere. But this one raccoon he had just blew me away. The animal had sense almost like a person! She knew I was afraid of her—her name was Dixie—and Billy just adored her. So one day, he was going off to school, and he told me to take care of Dixie for him. 'Let her out for just a little while today, because she's getting bigger now, and needs to be out for a while.' I told Billy that I had all sorts of things to do, and that I couldn't just be outside all day sitting with his raccoon! But I agreed to go out with her for a while, at least, and take her out one time, so I did.

"Well I took her out in the front yard, and next thing I knew, she had climbed a tree, and I couldn't get her to come down. And she goes up there on a high branch, crosses her arms, and just looks down at me, as if to say, *uh huh!* I knew I couldn't sit out here with Dixie all day, and so I went back inside. It wasn't even fifteen minutes after I'd gone back inside before I got a phone call, and it was one of the neighbors. She said, 'Glenda, is it your son that has the little raccoon?' I told her yes, and wanted to know why she was asking. She told me that the raccoon had just opened their screen door, and was now in their kitchen! Well I told him then that we'd have to do something with the raccoon, and that she couldn't just run loose or she might get us *all* in trouble. She stayed with us just a little while longer after that, before Billy finally turned her over to an animal shelter where they take in younger wild animals that had been injured and the like.

"There was one more animal that Billy and I had a bind about after Dixie the raccoon, and that was a snake. It was a pretty snake, with kind of a yellow and gold color. It was probably a corn snake, and a *very* large one, too. I told Billy that everything would be just fine, as long as the snake stayed in its big glass container. But then one day, Billy asked if he could go to the pet store over in town to get some mice. I didn't understand what he needed mice for, and when I asked him, he said, 'well I have to feed the snake.' I didn't like the idea, but I relented, and said that if he *had* to have them, that we would go get them. Well shortly after our trip, I walked by, and I saw that poor little mouse inside that terrarium, and it had its little feet up on a log, just like it was praying. The snake was just watching him, and I told Billy that this was just horrible. 'We're putting that snake out in the woods, and he can find his own food! I can't take seeing that little mouse in there, knowing that big snake is looking right at him.' It took some talking, but we finally convinced Billy, and the snake was returned to the woods. Believe me, it was turbulent."

Glenda also told me about the jobs Billy had worked as a young man, which included hard labor like roofing operation owned by his uncle. By the time he was about eighteen, he had been out on his own, and working full time under the family roofing business.

Granted, when Billy was much younger, he had suffered what doctors called a "severe strain" to the neck in a playground accident. Several years later, Billy and Glenda were stopped at a traffic light in town, and as they moved out slowly into traffic, a car pulled out from behind and moved quickly around them; as it passed, the front of Glenda's car only barely bumped the rear of the passing vehicle. "It wasn't a real severe hit, just enough to stop us. Billy sort of went forward and hit the dash, not severely, but enough that he said, 'I can't turn my neck!' Luckily, through the grace of God, there was an off-duty paramedic right in the car beside us. He came over and asked if he could look at my son, and I said of course. He put a neck brace on Billy, and told me he had already called 911.

"So when we got to the hospital, they kept Billy for a long time, and came out to ask me a lot of questions about when he was younger, and whether he had had any severe accidents. I said told them about the playground accident, and they agreed that this explained a lot about what they found. What had happened was that when he fell off the slide and sprained his neck, his bones were so small and fragile that they were pushed to the side, and the vertebra had been unstable. He grew up that way, and underneath the base of his brain, his vertebra was almost completely dislodged. But you could look at it like this; had the little car accident not happened, we might never have found the condition at all before any serious problems might occur. It could have drastically affected his vision, but most of all, his growth. It's almost like God had been trying to get our attention.

"But anyway, once Billy did get into the roofing business, that surgery from so many years before did give him problems. His doctor finally told him he would need to find another profession, because Billy was carrying huge, heavy loads of tiles up onto roofs and the like. It was hard work! But at that same time, he would work all day, and then come home and cook for his grandparents in the evenings. He was such a good boy.

"Then after that he went into department store management, and after that it was water resource management. He's still on the board with that company event today, while he's here running the mansion. When he and Michael got this place, I was a little worried that it would be more than they could handle. But they've really done a fine job. They learned all the history, and they had been finding out a lot. Getting a lot of info throughout the years that even I didn't know about. After the initial shock that they had bought a three-story mansion, I was thrilled."

❖   ❖   ❖

We were enjoying our talk, like a couple of old souls nestled together by a bonfire spinning yarns around shared memories, and before long, my conversation with the very accommodating Glenda Corsaro had begun to drift back around to items of interest yet again; namely having to do with the ghostly activity allegedly going on in Maggie's Room.

"When was your first visit here to the mansion?" I asked.

"It was after they got it up and going, and the first room I stayed in was," Glenda paused for a moment. "It was the one that has the entity in it."

"Maggie's room?" I said, surprised.

"Yes, that was the very first room I ever stayed in!" I had to admit I found it interesting, with a guest bedroom that had actually been named after Mrs. Corsaro, that Billy would have chosen Maggie's Room instead for her first night in the mansion.

"Did you have anything interesting happen?"

"My door wouldn't stay shut," she explained. "It never would stay shut. But I knew nothing about that room, they never told me a word about it until after they had been here a while. I had already stayed in that room, and I remember that first night I went upstairs, and I locked the door with the key they gave me. And when I got out of the shower and came into the room, the door was open!

"Now, my friend has a daughter who lives in New York, and she and Billy are very close. She was the photographer for the mansion, Shary Connella. Well she had stayed in that room, and so I asked her, "did you ever have trouble with the door in Maggie's Room? And she said, 'oh yeah I did. That door wouldn't stay shut!' So a lot of the people that have stayed in there have said that the door won't stay shut, even when they lock it."

"There are a lot of stories about that room," I replied, trying to be careful not to issue any leading questions on my own part. I asked again if this had been the main entrance to the room, which was immediately to the left at the top of the stairs, and Glenda agreed that it was the main entry door, which would mysteriously come open even when it had been shut and locked.

"Oh I've had other guests tell me that they've had their keys go missing from that room. They would look the entire room over, and in nearly every instance where a key went missing, it would appear later under the bed. One man said he had already looked beneath the bed more than once, and that it nearly startled him when he checked again and found the key lying there, in plain view! He said it was the weirdest thing he had ever seen."

"That's very interesting. Has anything else interesting like that ever happened while you've been staying here?" I asked.

"No, but I'll tell you this. I'm not afraid; I'm not afraid at all, and sometimes I do feel like there is something there, but I'm not afraid of it. We lived in a home that I think had a spirit."

"Really?"

"Yes, and it made noises, *lots* of noises. I never saw an entity or anything, but I did hear things." Finally, I asked Glenda if she had ever had anything she would consider to be extraordinary happen to here at all, here or elsewhere.

"I haven't, but certainly have spoken to guests staying here who say they have. And I know that one day, if I keep coming here, something will happen.

"I'm expecting it almost," Glenda said with a smile. "And when it happens, I don't think it will shock me at all."

MEANINGFUL COINCIDENCES

"What connexion can there have been between many people in the innumerable histories of this world, who, from opposite sides of great gulfs, have, nevertheless, been very curiously brought together!"

CHARLES DICKENS, "BLEAK HOUSE," 1852-53

SUNSET TRICKLED SLOW LIKE HONEY OVER THE HORIZON IN the distance, and from the porch of Reynolds Mansion, I watched the canvas of red, orange and grey spill across the sky ahead of me as I swirled melted ice in the bottom of my brandy glass, ceding to the beautiful indolence of the moment. I wished somehow to find a way to capture these seconds before twilight, to collect and store them away in some bundle that hid the essence of the day, perhaps to save for another evening with less natural promise and color than this one.

Tonight, I wished that the light of day receding behind the mountains in the distance might take with it the troubling questions that had haunted me since my arrival at the Reynolds family home. While they intrigued me, I nonetheless found myself consumed by their mystery. Even my dreams had been occupied by the house and its secrets; in one of these nighttime reveries, I found myself with a key to the place, and thinking it empty, entered to find it full of people I had known throughout my lifetime. I shuffled shoulder-to-shoulder past familiar faces, climbed the mansion's staircases, and made my way toward the building's upper levels; but soon realized that the modest three floors of the mansion I recognized continued further on, higher and higher up the ascending stairs, leading to hidden floors I had never known previously. I climbed higher, and upon reaching the apex, there were wide galleries with high ceilings, the likeness of some gothic cathedral in dark viridescent hues of olive green and mahogany. A massive veranda ran the entire length of the outside, and dark blue storm clouds whipped their chill against its stone balusters. What part of the Reynolds home was this, aside from some melancholy addition that had been built solely along the foundation that existed within my mind, and its contorted recollections of the outside world?

Within this large area at the summit of my haunted dreamscape, there were workers clad in white moving about with haste, busily preparing for some sort of event—a large masquerade or wedding, perhaps—and in the fervor of the moment, time hadn't seemed to grace any of these laborers with enough moments to spare discussing it with me. It goes without saying that dreams such as these are the stuff of symbolism, and can rarely be taken literally or at face value. Yet within my mind's recesses, I could very plainly see that the colors and essences of Reynolds Mansion were painting odd portraits in my mind, shaping characters and spaces that, while existent only in the psychic sense, nonetheless bore the same spirit of the old house whose halls I wandered in the waking hours.

Somehow, this place had spun the webs of its years around my mind, fastening my attention to its silken walls, and unreeling its mysteries around me like the gossamer threads of the spider, which leaves sleeping victims thread bound in its spindly kingdom, only to return later and devour them.

In the evenings, I would occasionally take to wandering the streets of this odd little mountain town that is Asheville, in order to help collect the thoughts of the day. Sometimes these evening ventures would last for hours. I would stroll by shops where art and paintings adorned the walls, and where spring flowers and mint leaves could be seen through the lighted windows. All the storefronts were quiet and empty this time of day, save maybe a late-night auction going on, or a fine restaurant where a foreign girl might come running to the door, recognizing the nighttime wander outside.

"Have you seen any aliens?" she asks cheerfully, knowing my interest in pursuing the unexplained. I tell her I hadn't, at least not tonight, but that if anything, maybe I was the alien.

Drifting along further into the night, I pass bars where singers and dancers played, and taverns where brothers, lovers and adversaries collected around table tops and dram glasses to sport the fare of social intoxication; the only medium safe enough for most people to have deep conversations anymore. I would carry along unnoticed outside, like a dark whisper on the breeze. I wander in silence, almost invisible, and watch the world go by as I stroll along aimlessly... dreaming of some bright afternoon with sunshine in great abundance, and lovely flowers ripe for picking.

During late-night romps like these, I often find myself imagining life the way it was in simpler times. I think of the days when Reynolds Mansion sat virtually alone on that mountainside across town, shielded from view by the mask of tall trunks of trees and dark shadows of the evening. I often consider the closeness and importance that family life had for people in those times. Reynolds Mansion hadn't only been a large building designed for aesthetic appeal; it was the family dwelling of one group of relatives for more than a century, colored by their visions and personalities, and despite no longer being occupied by the descendants of those pioneering families who built the place, it will forever remain a lasting testament to their way of life, their sense of purpose, and the important role the Reynolds family played in the founding and formation of this region. That mansion had long served as the foundation of their dreams, the culmination of their hopes and aspirations, and even today plays as aide-mémoire to the Reynolds legacy for all who enter.

These things tumbled along in my mind on this night, as I wandered Asheville's dampened city streets. I am one who has often been called an "old soul," and there are certainly nights, like this one, where I have indeed felt far removed from the present day. The expression of deep thought and consternation fitting my brow had drawn giggles from teenage girls as I trudged along in my contemplative promenade, oblivious to my own seriousness as I pondered the life and times of the Reynolds clan, and whether such possibilities as the existence of wayward spirits at the mansion today could truly be a reality. What is one to make of these sorts of tales about ghosts and the like? How is it that some are able to see the spirits of silent and long-dead ladies who lived there, while others—namely myself—remained oblivious to their coming and going, save only for echoes afforded me in tales from others who claim to have witnessed such odd, fascinating circumstances?

Could it really be so simple as the fact that no ghosts really existed there at all? Even Billy and Marti had shared stories where they felt, with certainty, that they too had seen things they couldn't explain. One evening, following a wedding that was held on the grounds earlier in the day, Marti and one of the other employees at the mansion named Jim had been straightening the house and preparing for breakfast the following morning. While there were still guests in the cottages adjacent to the house, no one had been allowed in the main building with them on this particular evening.

"I remember glancing up the staircase at one point," Marti would tell me later of the incident, "and thinking, *did I just see that?* It looked like someone's face had just darted right around the corner, peeking out at us, and then went right back." Marti began to ask Jim if he had seen anything, but before she could speak, his reaction had been the same, framing her own suspicions as he asked her about the same apparent apparition further up the staircase. No guests were to be allowed in the building at this hour; so who, or *what*, had been peering at them from the second floor?

Marti's daughter, Hannah, had also had an experience while staying at the mansion, which by comparison was probably more similar to some of my own encounters, in that it had taken place while she was staying in Maggie's Room. During the summer of 2012, Marti had been tasked with managing the Mansion while Billy and Michael were out of town on vacation. On one occasion she called me late in the afternoon to tell me Hannah would be coming home from college for the weekend, and that I should come spend the evening with them at Reynolds Mansion. My schedule would not permit a last minute visit, however; as it turns out, this may have been the one night I absolutely *needed* to be there.

Only a few weeks earlier, Marti had been visiting Riverside Cemetery in Asheville, where a number of the Reynolds family members have been buried over the years. Among the gravestones one will find not only the burial site of Senator Robert Rice Reynolds, but also his ancestor Daniel Reynolds, builder of the famous mansion that bears his namesake. Nearby, the modest grave of

Annie Lee Reynolds

Annie Lee Reynolds rests as a plain slab of moss-covered stone protruding from the ground. As is often the case with older graves, dirt and lichen had slowly covered Annie Lee's headstone over the years, and so during her visit, Marti decided to take the time to clean the grave. Removing all the lichen and soil ended up taking hours, but in her persistence, Marti managed to get the aging stone much cleaner looking; arguably, she had been the first to do so in what had to be a very long time.

Returning to the night of Hannah's stay at Reynolds Mansion, the weather had been so bad that, upon her arrival, the lights in the mansion began to flicker violently, just before the power in the building went out completely. "We were without power for about three hours," Marti told me. Moving through the house, Marti and Hannah retrieved flashlights kept on the backs of unused guestroom doors throughout the place, and retreated to the parlor downstairs to wait out the storm.

After talking with her mother by the fireplace for a couple of hours, it became evident that the storm would ensue regardless, and so Hannah elected to retire for the evening, with at least some hope of sleeping tonight. She ascended the stairway toward Maggie's room, where she planned to stay, and after preparing for bed she finally locked the door behind her and crawled under the covers.

Suddenly, Hannah felt the sheets on the bed jerk very slightly toward her right side; surely this had only been her imagination playing tricks? But within mere moments, the tugging occurred again, this time with the corner of her covers moving noticeably as an unseen resident seemed to lift them, as if tucking Hannah into bed. Her treatment had not been frightening; if anything, she felt comforted by the sensation of an older woman standing there, tucking her covers around her. Perhaps Annie Lee's spirit chose to act this way out of gratitude for her mother's noble actions only a few weeks earlier.

❖   ❖   ❖

Billy was no exception to having had experiences of his own, and like the others, told a number of unique stories about his countless hours spent alone in Reynolds Mansion. Several times when I would visit, I had recalled standing outside the rear entrance, and watching Billy exit the library where his desk was situated, he would head down the hallway to come greet me at the door. Without exception, Billy *always* kept his eyes to the ground as he walked along, as if to avoid looking directly into the tall mirror that faced the front entryway as he passed it.

"Billy," I finally asked one day. "Why do you keep your head down when you walk by that mirror?"

"Oh gosh, I won't ever look at it," he said a bit bashfully. "I've always heard that ghosts can show up in the reflection of mirrors, even when you don't see them in your normal line of sight, and so it's become habit for me to keep from looking in that mirror whenever I walk past it."

There might indeed be logic one could apply toward qualifying such beliefs. Reflective surfaces, after all, are gathering visible light, comprising one portion of the electromagnetic spectrum, and focusing it back outward into the environment. If we wanted to get speculative, we might consider whether the act of viewing visible light energy reflected off a surface (in other words, utilizing the mirrored surface as a sort of physical medium) could contribute to differences in the perception of certain things about a physical environment. While this sort of phenomenon certainly does not seem to be anything that is commonplace, given that such conditions might actually exist at all, we do know already that certain kinds of mirrors and filters can behave differently in terms of what varieties of light they reflect. Special mirrors known as *dichroic filters* can behave in such a way that visible light can be allowed to pass directly through them, while infrared light is reflected off their surface. These are more commonly referred to as "hot mirrors," and are used to prevent the build up of heat on electrical components and other areas by reflecting portions of the visible light spectrum that are unneeded for certain applications. All this to say, there are at least some instances where light as perceived by the naked eye, when compared with light reflected off the surface of a mirror, can vary in subtle ways. But even if we supposed that ghostly apparitions were operating within portions of, say for instance, the infrared realm as they manifested, it might still be difficult to say that this would cause them to appear more visibly in mirrors. On the other hand, it might certainly explain why strange apparitions are sometimes alleged to appear in photographs, since limited perception of the near-infrared realm has indeed become far more available to us in recent years, especially since the advent of digital cameras.

Perhaps a more likely explanation for some of the optical conditions mirrors can provide, which seem so conducive to spirit activity, has more to do with age-old practices such as scrying and mirror gazing. For centuries, various cultures have used reflective surfaces to elicit altered states of consciousness, where many have claimed to be able to communicate with the dead. The practice of divination using mirrors is generally referred to as *Catoptromancy*, and such practices were perhaps best represented in various rituals stemming from ancient Rome and Greece. One such early account, related by the ancient Greek traveler Pausanias, was described as follows:

> Before the Temple of Ceres at Patras, there was a fountain, separated from the temple by a wall, and there was an oracle, very truthful, not for all events, but for the sick only. The sick person let down a mirror, suspended by a thread till its base touched the surface of the water, having first prayed to the goddess and offered incense. Then looking in the mirror, he saw the presage of death or recovery, according as the face appeared fresh and healthy, or of a ghastly aspect.

We also find reference to the curious magic of reflective surfaces with regard to the Oracle of the Dead at Thesprotia, which dealt with a process referred to by scholars as the *nekyomanteion,* or it's modern variant, the *psychomanteum.* What this process entailed was a darkened room with a large, reflective surface, which initiates to sacred rituals would gaze into from a vantage where their own reflection could not be seen. Such practices have traditionally been used to evoke altered states among various spiritualist practices throughout the centuries. Even in modern times, psychologists the likes of Dr. Raymond Moody have claimed to effectively implement similar practices; in his 1993 book *Reunions,* Moody discussed the modern implementation of a psychomanteum for purposes of grief counseling those suffering from anxiety and depression, often associated with the death of a loved one.

There may still be other reasons for Billy's discomfort, however, with direct regard to the large mirror in the hallway outside guest room Lila. One woman visiting the mansion early after Billy and Michael opened to the public had stayed in Lila, and described having an odd late-night encounter with a spirit that not only manifested nearby, but also seemed to share a unique message with her.

"There was a very tall elderly man I saw in the room last night," the woman announced at breakfast the next morning. "When he appeared before me, I thought I was dreaming, but then he began to tell me he was upset because the door over in the corner of the room was locked." Stories dating back several decades also mention this particular door joining guest room Lila— once the master bedroom of Daniel Reynolds—with the library next to it.

"She didn't know anything about those stories about the door," Billy told me excitedly of the woman's encounter. "She was just a guest!"

Billy had also had one fleeting experience, which he stopped just short of calling an encounter, that took place in the hallway outside Lila. "The only time that I ever thought I saw something myself in the house—and I don't really know if it could have just been my imagination—but I was standing here in the hallway, just outside Lila. I was winding up the chord to the vacuum, and out of the corner of my eye, standing right here by this mirror, I saw a very tall man. He had a beard, and was wearing a tan waistcoat that came very low," Billy said, gesturing with his hand to show the approximate length of the coat. "I jumped, because I saw it out of my peripheral vision. And the man wasn't there after I had jumped like that. But I said aloud, standing there by myself, *my God, I think I just saw a ghost!* It did really frighten me."

Billy's sighting of what appeared to be an apparition in his peripheral vision is also a common circumstance when it comes to stories taking place in haunted houses. Many who report seeing ghosts and apparitions will state that what they had seen appeared "out of the corner of my eye," much like Billy described. Again, this sort of circumstance may have something to do with the possibility that certain apparitional manifestations are occurring outside the normal jurisdictions of visible light; and interestingly, there may also be physical reasons underlying why some people report seeing ghosts in this manner.

Beginning in the 15th century during Japan's Sengoku period, historic references to the *Shinobi,* which were essentially ninja mercenaries, began to appear. These stealth warriors would incorporate a variety of different techniques for purposes of spying and espionage, among them the stereotypical dark garb for purposes of moving unseen by night. However, for one to be able to move effectively in darkness, it helps to also be able to *see* in darkness too. Quite obviously, night vision technologies would not begin to appear, even in their infancy, for another several hundred years; but the Shinobi, being resourceful as they were, may have begun to utilize other natural processes to help move past the complications that a demand for night-vision entailed. According to ninjutsu historian and author Ashida Kim, these medieval ninja warriors had learned that an improved ability to see in near-darkness could be achieved by cultivating sight in the eye's periphery. Prior to a stealth operation by cover of darkness, the ninja were said to allow several minutes for their eyes to adjust completely to darkness. Then, as they began to move about, they would employ this night-vision technique, looking just to the side of an object or area they were viewing in near darkness, allowing their peripheral vision to help them better recognize their surroundings.

It is interesting that the ninja would stumble onto such a useful technique by the fifteenth century, since in modern times we know that the greatest concentration of rod cells within the retina exist around its outer edges. These particular cells, rather than being capable of recognizing color like their cousins, the cone cells, are better suited for vision in low-light settings. Thus, the physical reasons underlying one's strongest low-light vision existing in the periphery becomes apparent.

Taking this one step further, we know that a variety of animals, including domestic pets like dogs and cats, are far better equipped with night vision than humans. Such heightened natural abilities have long served members of the animal kingdom who evolved to survive as nocturnal hunters; interestingly, we also hear a variety of stories where pets living with people in homes alleged to be haunted are described as having a better ability to perceive the realms beyond. Again, this brings to mind the potential for certain electromagnetic aspects of spiritual phenomenon manifesting within the infrared portion of the spectrum; if this assumption were accurate, it might explain why not only animals seem to be able to perceive ghostly phenomenon more readily than humans, but also why people often claim to see apparitional forms with their peripheral vision.

I would come to find that there were still other parallels that existed with regard to the appearances of a tall, bearded man here at Reynolds Mansion, some of which became of direct personal relevance to my own experiences here. I was told that on one occasion, Jess had been upstairs in guest room Vera, polishing a mirror that hung on the wall directly adjacent to the main doorway. Again, from the corner of her eye, she very clearly saw in the mirror's reflection that a tall man was standing behind her, over by the entrance to the bathroom. Jess had hardly been given time to become startled, and turned to address the man instead, believing him to be one of the guests that weekend.

"I'm sorry, can I help you sir?" she started to say, but turning to face the doorway behind her, there was, of course, no man to be seen.

The man, according to Jess, had been tall and elderly, very thin, and sporting gray facial hair, much like the apparition seen in the downstairs portion of the building. But in all fairness, I had to accept that the description Jess had given also matched, with near perfection, the features of an elderly man I had witnessed in what I could only refer to as a "vision," where he lay in the old claw foot tub of Vera's darkened bathroom during my first visit at the mansion. For obvious reasons, I had initially elected to keep this story to myself; I had seen no apparition, but instead had only "seen" the man lying there in my imagination, as though something about the surroundings had prompted or *triggered* the image in my mind's eye. While the sensation this experience managed to draw for me was very strong, and even disturbing, I elected to keep the experience to myself, assuming that although it had carried an emotional impact at the time, it might prove to be less significant in hindsight. If anything, hearing Jess's story now seemed to lend a bit of credence to these circumstances, which up to that point I had hoped I merely imagined.

"You mean to tell me that you saw something up there in Vera also?"

Marti sat looking at me with an excited expression on her face, as though she could at any moment leap from her chair across the library. "And you never told anyone about this?"

"Well Marti, again I have to say that I didn't *see* the man. It was more like I had an image appear in my mind, as I entered the bathroom right there by the bed."

Marti just shook her head. "Amazing," she finally said. "Now tell me about this. Tell me *all about it.*"

I recounted the experience for her, noting that there were obviously a number of similarities between what Jess had described seeing and my own encounter, though I still hardly felt comfortable calling it an "encounter" of any kind.

"Maybe it's really just a meaningful coincidence," I offered. This summary seemed most fitting to me, since it is in essence the definition for what psychologist Carl Jung referred to as *synchronicity*. While Jung was the first to initiate discussion of meaningful coincidences using this terminology, others have gone on to build on the idea; in his book *Synchronicity: The Art of Coincidence, Choice, and Unlocking Your Mind*, Dr. Kirby Surprise supposes that one can not only learn to develop an ability to use such things as synchronicity to one's advantage, but that harnessing this might literally constitute, "learning to think outside the box of space-time."

I've never claimed to be anyone who professed having psychic abilities. However, there are times in most anyone's life where certain events and circumstances seem to be far more meaningful and interrelated than what can be explained through mere coincidence. In fact, some of the events leading to the lasting bond of friendship that grew between Marti Marfia and I seemed to involve an occurrence of this sort. Several years ago, I had gone through a particularly bad breakup, and though we weren't necessarily close or in regular contact at the time, Marti had known me through a mutual friend of ours, and would call every now and then just to touch base and say hello. Within two days of my breakup, I not only received a phone call from Marti, but also a concerned inquiry from her about my wellbeing.

When the phone call arrived, she explained that within the last day or so, I had been very prominently on her mind, and that she had the worst feeling that something terrible may have happened in my life. Needless to say, I was a bit surprised to hear this, and thus decided to explain the circumstances to Marti in greater detail. A mother of two girls, one in her early teens at the time, the other preparing to leave for college, Marti's understanding of relationship troubles proved to be a sincere blessing during that period. But one thing I'd never gotten over had been her apparent ability to sense that I had been going through emotional hardship at the time. How had she known, and for that matter, how *could she have known?* I had asked her, point blank, whether somebody might have alluded to there being a breakup, but Marti insisted that in addition to having no prior knowledge of what had happened, she also had not been in contact with anyone who could have supplied her with that information. It might be one thing if Marti had ever shown a tendency to exaggerate or blow things out of proportion over the years. But if anything, she had become one of the most consistent, rock-solid individuals I knew in terms of trustworthiness and reliability, and well in advance of our dealings together in more recent times at Reynolds Mansion.

Therefore, it seemed only fitting that when these *synchronicities*—for lack of any better term—began to envelop my life shortly after undertaking study of Reynolds Mansion and its history, Marti became the first person I chose to discuss matters with in depth. We decided it might be fitting for a change, rather than barricading ourselves in the Reynolds library this time, to go antique hunting instead, and discuss our unusual matters in the presence of other old spirits. We arrived at the Antique Tobacco Barn on Swannanoa River Road a little before noon on a drizzly Saturday afternoon. I was running late, having stopped to get coffee for our rainy day expedition, but soon we were wandering along, dodging between ancient antique cupboards and closets, many the likes of which could have lived happily in a place like Reynolds Mansion.

"Marti, these sorts of things are literally happening every day at this point," I told her. "I don't know why, but I keep having all these meaningful coincidences, and some of them almost defy explanation."

"Well you've gotta give me an idea what you mean first," she laughed. "What kinds of things have happened?"

One instance that came immediately to mind had occurred a few weeks beforehand, during a rare opportunity for lounging that transpired early one Sunday afternoon. While lying on the couch, gazing out the window, I remember an odd and decidedly random image from my childhood coming to mind. Growing up, my father had been the rector at an Episcopal church within just a few miles of Reynolds Mansion, and on Sunday afternoons following the church services, my younger brother and I would often play with the other children who attended, roaming the grounds and, occasionally, the graveyard that stood on the hill above the sanctuary. There had been an older couple that attended there for a number of years, Mitchell and Eileen Buckner, and I always found it strange that what I took to be a headstone had existed behind the church, on with both their names were inscribed. Had they secured their grave markers well in advance, perhaps in the event that the onset of poor health might cause a turn for the worse at some point? I knew that Mitchell's physical condition had begun to decline steadily several years back, prompting a number of surgeries. For whatever reason this all came to mind, it suddenly had me wondering how Mitchell was doing now. After all, it had been years since I had seen the man, and in truth, probably years since he had even crossed my mind. With that, the image of the gravestone in my mind had come and gone with little more thought given to the matter.

The following day, I had arranged to have my parents drop in for breakfast, and I had busily been working at getting our meal prepared when I managed to burn my finger on a hotplate just as my company arrived. Needless to say, they entered my kitchen to find a rather comical scene: here I was spooning fruit compote and scrambled eggs into dishes, one handed, while my other hand carried a juice glass full of ice water, in which the burned forefinger had been submerged. At that moment, I remember my mother running to get orange juice and a breakfast salad from the refrigerator, as my father removed his hat with an exhausted expression on his face.

"We just found out Mitchell Buckner died yesterday," he said.

"Really?" I replied, obviously a bit saddened, and immediately noting the personal coincidence this represented for me, albeit privately. I asked around what time it was thought that the death occurred, and my father told me it had been sometime early in the afternoon the previous day.

It would be several weeks before I finally told my parents about the coincidence, while visiting their home for dinner one evening. I explained the circumstances to them, and my father, known to be a bit skeptical at times, listened to my story with an impartial expression on his face. I described the memory of seeing Mitchell Buckner's name inscribed on the headstone, and how this had suddenly entered my mind at around one in the afternoon on the same day Mitchell would have passed away.

"Ah ha!" Dad exclaimed. "But that's where you're wrong!"

"Had he not died on that same Sunday afternoon?" I asked.

"Oh no, he did," Dad replied. "And it must have been around the same time you had that image cross your mind. Sometime between one and two o'clock."

"Well how was I wrong, then?" I asked a bit perturbed.

"There was no grave stone behind the church," he said.

"Impossible," I argued. "I remember it being there, and having their names on it. What else could I have seen?"

"That wasn't a gravestone behind the sanctuary," he maintained. "It was a commemorative plaque; *that's* what you remember seeing."

So in essence, I *had* been right, and at virtually the same time Mitchell Buckner had passed away, I received an otherwise very random image of what I had at least mistaken to be a headstone bearing his name. Excusing the fact that this object I had always thought to be a grave marker was actually a memorial plaque, I thought the circumstances had otherwise been quite noteworthy.

While I couldn't be certain that any of these sorts of experiences I had been having were directly related to the goings on at Reynolds Mansion, they did cause me to revisit the incident that had taken place several weeks beforehand in guest room Vera. Maybe I wasn't any more prone to experiencing these sorts of "meaningful coincidences" than anyone else; and yet, to ignore such things outright would almost have seemed an injustice, all things considered. I had great difficulty divorcing myself from the possibility that certain events or aspects of the historic past could occasionally spill over into our present reality; and that the elements making this sort of thing possible might very well exist outside our conventional understanding of the sciences today.

I was, of course, far from being the only person thinking about Reynolds Mansion and its oddities along these lines. On many occasions, Billy and I had shared long conversations about what physical forces could allow the ghosts of decades, and even *centuries* past, to cross the boundaries of time in such a way that allowed them to interact with our present reality.

"I've wondered if actual instances of parallel time could exist," Billy suggested to me one afternoon in a lull between checking in guest arrivals. "I don't look at time as being just one-dimensional, or one-directional for that matter. I think that sometimes time as we know it gets bunched up, and when conditions are right, it might even overlap with itself for short periods of time."

"Billy, do you recall *A Wrinkle in Time,* the book by Madeline L'Engle?" I remembered reading this book as a child in elementary school, and even at that early age finding the author's discussion of such things as *tesseracts*—a variety of fourth-dimensional construct referenced throughout the novel—completely enthralling.

"There was a great analogy for the very sort of thing you're describing," added. "I remember reading that book as a child, and seeing a diagram where bending time in order to bring two distant points together was likened to an ant crawling across a length of string. If the string represented space-time, and the ant wished to leap across a great span in a shorter period, it could be done so by bringing the two ends of the string together, allowing the middle portion to droop between them. Now, the ant could still leave from his original starting place, but arrive at his destination in a single step."

"Precisely," Billy agreed. "We don't know how it might happen, but I think about this sort of thing all the time, and how those very sorts of things could be taking place within the walls of this home. Just because we don't know how it happens, doesn't mean at all that it *couldn't happen.* These things aren't for naught."

I had long been considering ways we might be able to gather information during our visits at Reynolds Mansion which, in addition to the wealth of photos, documents, and other historical data we had already uncovered, might help us to learn more about the supernatural phenomenon taking place here. While my views would no doubt draw opposition from many in the "paranormal" community, I had become somewhat vexed with the modern methods of ghost hunting, which involved the assortment of electromagnetic field meters, cameras and night-vision camcorders, and other tools believed to aid in the discovery of spirit presences within a given locale. As I have discussed previously, it often seems to be the case that, while these sorts of tools could indeed be capable of measuring various things related to ghostly energies, we are still left more or less incapable of doing much with this sort of data. In other words, we often presuppose things like, "a ghost is the spirit of a dead person," and furthermore, that the energies that must constitute that disembodied spirit must be measureable using, of all things, devices that were made to find electromagnetic "pollution" in an environment, given off by manmade objects. Then this sort of "data" is used as evidence for some great misfortune that might have taken place long ago in the given locale. Sure, all of these things might be relevant to understanding ghostly phenomenon; but it becomes evident that a lot of gaps in logic do begin to emerge also, as well as what amounts to little more than wishful thinking, and fanciful stories woven around the expectations of the would-be paranormalist.

I wasn't the only one who expressed having misgivings about the science of ghost hunting, especially as it related to occurrences at Reynolds Mansion. Billy confided in me that a handful of paranormal investigation groups had visited the mansion, typically requesting that they be allowed to carry out their research by cover of night, typically between midnight and around three in the morning. Billy had always disliked that aspect of the ghost hunting process as an innkeeper, since his title required him to be an early riser each morning.

"But to be honest, most of the activity that people report occurs in the daytime. Almost all the really good stories of people seeing apparitions in this house have taken place between around two and four in the afternoon." Billy seemed a bit troubled by this facet of the mystery, though perhaps more so by the fact that the visiting investigative groups would almost always overlook it. With time, and the passage of many conversations about the philosophy of ghost hunting, Billy would begin to rely on me to act as a sort of "screener" for the various groups that contacted him about performing investigations at the place.

But despite my own feelings about ghost research, there were at least a few areas where I found there to be certain merit. For instance, the study of electronic voice phenomenon, or EVP as it is more often called, had in at least a few cases seemed to present incredible evidence of voices being captured on recordings in various places alleged to be haunted. While we hadn't managed to detect any ethereal crosstalk of this sort during our remote broadcast at the mansion a few weeks earlier, Chris Heyes and I nonetheless thought it might be interesting to try our hand at recording segments of audio in a few of the more "active" rooms throughout the house, with the intention of asking certain key questions that might garner the sorts of responses one would hope to hear from a ghost.

Chris joined me later that afternoon, and after wrapping up our discussion with Billy in the dining room, we left him to the business of afternoon check-ins as we ascended toward the third floor. Strange though it was that so much of the bumping and thumping of haunted activity seemed to emanate from the third floor of the building (which had been added on much later during the renovations Nat Augustus Reynolds completed close to a century ago), we decided to begin our EVP session in Maggie's Room, where Annie Lee's wayward spirit was supposed to have lingered with moderate frequency. We continued along next to Vera, the location of my own initial psychic disturbance in the house, and then descending to the lower floors, performed the same process in guest rooms Claudette, Lila, and a few others.

Our questions had been rather formulaic, based on an outline I had designed specifically for the session, in which Chris and I first introduced ourselves by name and profession, and described what the devices we were carrying with us were designed to do. Once introductions were out of the way, we would move on to asking questions that, if any presence in our midst felt comfortable answering, were designed to gain access to information such as what era or year it might be, relative to the perspective of any being or entity which may answer. We also asked for any present entities to state their names, why they were here at Reynolds Mansion, and whether they had any information they felt should be passed along to us.

Chris and I elected to use an MXL BCD-1 Dynamic Broadcast Microphone for this experiment, which is designed to work via electromagnetic induction. An interesting experiment had been shown to me a few years earlier by a colleague of mine, Joshua P. Warren, which solidified in my mind how dynamic microphones of this sort might be far more useful in gathering information through the presence of electromagnetic anomalies than conventional EM detectors. In essence, Joshua had disconnected the speakers from a stereo system, and instead attached to the stereo outputs a cable that sent the electronic signal to a large copper coil, which had seen years of use in laboratory experiments. The large coil produced no audible sounds, of course, but the electronic information was carried from the stereo nonetheless, and broadcast silently as an electromagnetic field emanating from the copper coil. Here's where things began to get interesting: while the human ear could discern no noise, if one were to hold a dynamic microphone connected to a recording device next to the coil, the EM field being broadcast would resonate with the coil inside the microphone. On playback of the recorded audio, the sounds normally carried by the stereo speakers, though inaudible to the human ear when "broadcast" in this way, can be heard quite clearly on the recording. In other words, we might posit that certain electromagnetic energies present in an environment could carry information that our ears are incapable of discerning on their own, but which nonetheless become audible when recorded using the appropriate kinds of equipment.

We spent the next couple of hours conducting our vigil, recording long periods of silence between targeted questions in the various rooms of the house. Billy joined us for our session in guest room Lila, and once we had completed our survey, I saved the various audio files and we made our exit. It was several days before I had enough spare time to analyze, enhance, and study the various audio segments. I listened and re-listened to each portion of audio from the individual rooms, carefully highlighting large swathes of silence and boosting the volume levels considerably with my audio editing software. I also applied various filters, to reduce or, at times, increase the audible hiss in a given environment, to see if I could bring out or separate any unusual sounds or other anomalies. Then I repeated this entire painstaking process, waited a few days, and tried it all again, but to no avail. There simply did not seem to be anything resembling a vocalized response to any of my questions during our EVP session.

While I had begun to grow frustrated with the lack of information that had been forthcoming, at least in the spiritualist sense, I was not yet discouraged. I was, however, becoming even further convinced that, while under some circumstances there may be merit to the use of scientific equipment in determining the cause of a haunting, this may not be one of them. Unless, of course, I had been prepared to accept that there simply were no ghosts at Reynolds Mansion, and that the lack of evidence thus far spoke for itself. This was not a possibility I could rule out, despite any romantic appeal the idea of ghosts in our midst might have offered.

Perhaps a new approach was in order instead. The same summer I had begun my investigations at Reynolds Mansion, I had been asked by my publishers in New York, New Page Books, to pen an essay on parapsychology and ghost research for an anthology they released a few months later titled *Ghosts, Spirits, and Hauntings: Am I Being Haunted?* My essay was titled, "Psychic Gift or Psychotic Nightmare? The Biology of the Supernatural." However, in this same collection of essays on the science and study of paranormal phenomenon, another essay, written by veteran researcher Andrew Nichols, had managed to capture my attention, titled "Haunted Houses: Theaters of the Mind." In it, Nichols seemed to summarize my own attitudes toward more conventional modern approaches to ghost hunting:

> For too long, most paranormal investigators... have concentrated on the technological approach to haunting investigations, focusing on the use of various pieces and types of recording equipment with, frankly, very limited results. What has often been overlooked in the past has been the psychological aspect of hauntings, and that is because the haunted house still remains the domain of the amateur investigator, while most professional parapsychologists are more concerned with repeatable [psychokinesis] and ESP experiments in their laboratories and academic settings. This is

unfortunate because with a cooperative effort, we have a greater chance of reaching a better understanding of hauntings. The amateur ghost hunters also do not seem to be coming up with the goods, tending instead to stick with the same old concept of spirits.

Nichols outlined several of his observations regarding the parapsychological nature of ghosts and hauntings, and in particular, the use of what he called a "psi session" to stimulate subconscious responses from those in a haunted environment. In essence, the psi session would operate much like the nineteenth century séance, in which participants might utilize various activities such as automatic writing, table tilting, pendulums, or Ouija boards to extract information about the underlying occurrences, and regardless of whether that information seemed to stem from psychic sources in the environment, or from the very individuals who claimed to be experiencing aspects of the haunting themselves. From a psychological perspective, Nichols felt that using such processes allowed one the ability to employ a hypnotherapeutic technique known as *reframing*, in which subconscious influences could be used to change certain kinds of behavior or thought in an individual. In many of the more troubling investigations he had performed over the years, Nichols claimed that this technique had been quite useful in removing the disturbances and effectively "de-haunting" houses.

This avenue of thought called to mind another interesting question regarding the nature of any presumed haunting: for all we know, it is possible that various strange phenomena could use individuals as the medium by which they manifest. Indeed, this may point to a psychological source underlying the phenomenon, the likes of which psychologist Carl Jung might have called *exteriorized autonomous complexes* or *catalytic exteriorizations*. Interestingly, even Jung himself described seeing ghosts many times throughout his life, in addition to having experienced a variety of other strange circumstances. In fact, following the publication of a private memoir known as *The Red Book,* it became evident that Jung himself had engaged in a strange series of experiments in which he had induced hypnotic mental states very rich with symbolism, from which he believed he had been capable of deducing information from the human collective unconscious, utilizing a variety of mythic imagery he referred to as "archetypes." These experiments Jung conducted were in many ways quite similar to séances themselves, of which Jung later wrote the following:

> The years... when I pursued the inner images, were the most important time of my life. Everything else is to be derived from this. It began at that time, and the later details hardly matter anymore. My entire life consisted in elaborating what had burst forth from the unconscious and flooded me like an enigmatic stream and threatened to break me. That was the stuff and material for more than only one life. Everything later was merely the outer classification, scientific elaboration, and the integration into life. But the numinous beginning, which contained everything, was then.

Indeed, it may be the case that rather than seeking to find common ground through direct encounters with spirit presences at Reynolds Mansion, perhaps there were more subtle ways such things could be achieved. Maybe the fertile playground that is the human mind would provide a better medium for the exchange of such non-temporal discourse, as it had for Andrew Nichols, Carl

Jung, and a handful of others who sought to look past the blunt appeal of gadgetry, and favoring instead the psychological elements underlying strange phenomena.

A new hope for establishing contact between this state of being, and that which spirits like Annie Lee Reynolds may inhabit, seemed almost within reach at this point; but how we would seek to undertake this next most critical stage of study at Reynolds Mansion indeed would call for curious and potentially frightening new measures.

Plans for holding the first séance at Reynolds Mansion were now in order.

Nine

VOICES IN THE DARKNESS

"This night at Collinwood may prove to be the most terrifying, for this is the night that the living will try to contact the dead. Preparations are underway for that moment... the moment that one world will reach out to the other: a séance."

DARK SHADOWS, EPISODE 170, AIRED 17 FEBRUARY 1967

AS ONE ENTERS THE LIBRARY ON THE GROUND FLOOR OF Reynolds Mansion, above the desk in the corner hangs an antique portrait of the United States' Civil War-era Commander in Chief, Abraham Lincoln. Ranking high among the stranger film renditions afforded Honest Abe over the decades, his bizarre fictional portrayal as a vampire hunter in recent years saw the likeness of America's sixteenth President fitted with sharpened stakes and the various other accoutrements used to thwart denizens of the undead. While in his real existence Mr. Lincoln had never displayed

203

much interest in the study of vampires, there were nonetheless other realms of the occult that did capture his fancy, and no less for their associations with those who continue on after their physical bodies no longer remain.

Following the death of his sons Edward and, later on, Willie in 1862, Lincoln had not only seemed to rely on hope for an afterlife from which to draw comfort for his losses, but also in the existence of some medium through which his lost boys might be reached from within the mortal realm. Thus, during his tenure at the White House, Lincoln's wife, Mary Todd, was known to have organized séances that the President himself attended, held for just such purposes.

Indeed, the séance has long been viewed as a potential method for communicating with spirits. While conversing with the dead has a long and complex history throughout the cultures of the world, author and spiritualist Raymond Buckland notes in his book *Solitary Séance* that modern spirit communication in the West began under circumstances that were largely similar to those which have taken place at Reynolds Mansion for years now:

> In the early 1800s, as in previous centuries, many people heard "ghostly noises": banging and thumping, scratching and scraping. In Hydesville, New York, on March 31, 1848, a "conversation" developed, which is hailed as the birth of Modern Spiritualism. Later, others took the same approach and found that they too were able to exchange information with contacting spirits. Spirit communication became a movement and then a religion—one that is thriving today.

Indeed, while the art of spirit communication may not see the popularity it once did, it has never quiet died out either, as evidenced by the mass production of such things as Ouija boards, pendulums, and other tools for reaching separate realms of existence beyond the physical. In the Spiritualist tradition, it is commonly believed that such things can indeed allow access to other realms, where spirits of the deceased may establish contact with the living. Even in the technological era we now live in, claims have been made over the years that spirit communication has occurred through electronic mediums just as well; much like the electronic voice phenomenon discussed in earlier chapters, there have been various claims in more recent years that involve spirit messages being received through email correspondence, or even telephone calls. Despite one's preferred medium, the general belief that spirits can find means by which to reach the living has indeed persisted.

While my objective with plans for holding a séance at Reynolds Mansion had obviously been aimed at seeing if anything unusual or otherworldly might occur along these lines, there were other reasons the idea had held certain appeal as well. For one, Andrew Nichols had outlined the way that the process of holding séances could actually help one learn more about the living participants in question, in a psychological sense, rather than any ghosts one might hope to contact. In order to maintain objectivity, I was careful when it came to providing much commentary about this aspect of the experiment to those who planned to attend, so as not to influence their actions or perceptions of any events that might transpire.

Another reason the idea seemed appealing had been rooted in those earlier episodes of the *Dark Shadows* television program from the late 1960s, where the characters at Collinwood decided to hold a séance for purposes of contacting the spirit of Josette Du Press, the former lover of the vampire Barnabas Collins, whose spirit had remained there at the ancestral home in Collinsport. While this particular series of events had helped inspire the idea of holding a séance at Reynolds Mansion, beyond this inspiration it was not an aspect of the present circumstances that I took very seriously; still, the manner in which the theatrical séance had been conducted (which included a tape recording being made throughout) had at least been useful in formulating ideas as to how we might proceed with our own psychic experiment. Thus, in addition to performing the séance I had scheduled, I decided we would record audio during our session just as well.

And then there was the actual potential that existed, however remote it may have been, that we might establish legitimate communication of some variety, perhaps with some remnant consciousness of a former resident at the mansion. Even given these terms, I still found myself hesitant to call this form of "communication" actual discourse with a ghost or spirit. In my view, the multi-leveled complexity of the human mind simply makes it too difficult to discern precisely what may be going on during such feats as channeling, mediumship, or spirit talking by other methods. While my skepticism is obvious in this regard, I am also careful enough not to commit to belief favoring the opposite extreme either; in other words, I won't assume that a person who has claimed to perform in such a capacity is always simply buying their own hype, or worse, "performing" in such a way with the sole purpose of pulling the wool over the eyes of the gullible in our midst.

Despite my own care in going about the entire thing, there were still occasions during the planning stages where I had been met with resistance. My religious background had been an interesting one growing up; my father is an Episcopal priest, and thus I had received what one might call a fairly traditional Christian upbringing. By the same token, though he was often more skeptical with his attitudes even than I was, to this day my father keeps a very open mind to possibilities that exist in realms beyond the conventional areas where the modern religious mind would typically ever tread. Thus, while he expressed little interest in the idea of ghosts or spirit communication, he had nonetheless refrained from labeling such things as being "evil" or otherwise bad or mischievous in some way. My mother, on the other hand, had shown far more opposition to the idea as we discussed it over dinner one evening in the weeks leading up to our session at Reynolds Mansion. As it turned out, one of the listeners of my radio program had taken time to mail his Ouija board to us, granted that we return it to him with my signature added to its front, as he had been collecting the autographs of various individuals involved in the esoteric and paranormal fields. Making conversation, I had suggested the idea that I keep the item only long enough to employ its use during our experiment at Reynolds Mansion; this idea was not well received.

"Micah, you don't need to be messing with Ouija boards," she blurted out. "Those things can open doors to things and places that you won't be able to shut off!"

"Well," I began. "My own view regarding Ouija boards is that they rely on something called auto-motor response. There are tiny muscular movements that occur, even on a level that people can't perceive, that influence the way Ouija boards and other items used for divination behave."

My mother's apprehension toward Ouija boards drew from an experience she had as a teenager, during which she described receiving a startling amount of information about a young man who was allegedly killed in an automobile accident in the 1950s. As the story went, he had been driving a convertible when he lost control and ran off the side of a bridge; as he and his car fell into the water, he was pinned beneath the car, and couldn't escape drowning. The story had seemed so real to my mother, based on the questions she and her friend had been asking through the movement of the planchette across the front of the Ouija board, that the two became terrified of what was happening, and decided to end their discourse with the spirit world, once and for all. Although she has always maintained an interest in the supernatural, my mother has never again used Oujia boards for purposes of contacting the dead.

"You don't need to use them either," she warned me sternly. "They aren't good things to have around you!"

Of course, there are plenty of other practices that spiritualists over the years have employed during séances. For one, a process called "table tipping" had seemed appealing just as well; especially given the amount of old, antique furniture at Reynolds Mansion. This process involves the use of a small table, typically a wooden one fitted with three or four legs, which participants place their hands on top of, often with the tips of their little fingers touching, which completes a circle around the surface of the table. The person leading the séance will begin to ask questions, defining various ways that the table can tip or move to indicate things such as "yes" and "no." In some varieties, the table itself actually turns or tilts in accordance with spoken letters of the alphabet, hence the common use of an alternate term, known as "table turning." In this way, letters and phrases can be spelled out using a small table, which works similar to the function of Oujia boards.

Another spiritualist tool that can be employed easily is the pendulum. In this instance, a small object is suspended in midair by a short length of string, which is held between the thumb and forefinger of the participant. Questions are asked, and the movement of the pendulum will again serve in providing answers, typically through a back and forth movement meaning "yes," and a circular movement meaning "no," or vice versa, depending on the desired designation for use in determining answers to various questions. As one can plainly see, especially in the case of the pendulum, there is subtle movement that an individual's muscles will undergo. While this motion is so miniscule that the person whose muscles are twitching in this manner will be unaware of it, this is nonetheless the very obvious source of influence over the swinging weight. Hence, while we cannot say that the pendulum is *really* being taken and moved by some supernatural force, we might hazard to guess that our focus on the workings of the mind in any such instance becomes all the more important.

Thus, the conventional model here supposes that a person's own psyche influences the movements of a planchette across a Ouija board, the tilting of a table, or the swinging of a pendulum in a séance. Still, I couldn't help but also consider what kinds of subversive influences on our minds might nonetheless have the effect of providing seemingly supernatural "answers" to life's questions. At times, it seems rather difficult to discern what, or where, such information is really coming from.

The actual scheduling of the séance became a daunting task unto itself, and in the weeks leading up to the occasion, I found that I was met with continued mishaps. My first two attempts at securing a date for the experiment had to be canceled due to various other professional obligations, though we finally did manage to lock in a date for the evening of September 18, 2012. Then there had been the question of personnel; I had initially hoped that Marti, Billy, and I would serve as our "core group" for the experiment, although I hoped to add at least three others to help round things out, and provide a healthy number of individuals that would still be manageable, especially in the event that there were guests in attendance elsewhere in the mansion. I had also been counting on my assistant, Susan Davidson, being available to attend, especially since she has a rich background in working with psychics, remote viewing specialists, and a number of others who claimed to have supernatural prowess of one sort or another.

However, after our various schedule changes, the final date we resolved to hold the séance happened to also be Susan's birthday, and hence she was obligated to take her husband's offer to attend a family dinner with their two boys instead. For obvious reasons, I urged her to take him up on this, and assured her that she was indeed "off the hook," at least for this occasion.

On the morning of the 18th, even more bad luck began to ensue. Early in the day, I awoke to find myself feeling strange and dizzy. While I had been just fine only the night before, I now seemed to be suffering from odd temperature increases, which lasted all morning, accompanied by profuse sweating. I went about my business all the same, determined at this point that, as they famously have quipped in showbiz for decades already, "the show must go on." Then, as if to add further impetus behind the forces that seemingly wished to prevent our séance from taking place, I received news from Marti that Billy had unfortunately also been called away at the last minute; since it was a professional matter, he regretted that he would now be unable to join the rest of us for the séance that evening. At very least, we would not be required to change dates a third time, and having assumed there might be a necessity for technical help on-site, I had already enlisted the assistance of Matt and Chris, who would both participate in the séance itself, as well as manage audio equipment we would use to document the proceedings. Still, in the absence of Susan Davidson or any other females, this would leave us with three young gentlemen of a rather skeptical disposition, and one vibrant redhead who, despite all her apparent psychic prowess, nonetheless could suffer dilution due to all the testosterone present in the room. For success, I felt strongly that we needed to maintain a finer balance between male and female energies; was there not one other lady who could join us, let alone one who was both wise and brave enough to compliment an occasion so sensitive as this?

Only one other individual came to mind, though getting her would be a long shot. During the early spring of 2012, I had begun to experience a very strange set of circumstances with a friend of mine, who at the time was really barely more than an acquaintance, named Lisa Northrup. As a musician by trade, in addition to my more macabre fascinations, it was during a weekly bluegrass performance I began doing Wednesday evenings in Highlands, North Carolina in the winter of 2010 that Lisa and I had become acquainted. Some time during the summer of the following year, she invited me to join her for cocktails at her home prior to a performance I did on a Friday evening. This would be our first and only date, and for various reasons the two of us more or less fell out of touch in the months that followed, despite there being an obvious, though at times *unusual* attraction between us.

Our mutual esoteric interests would nonetheless lead to a rekindling of our desire for conversation after several more months, and as we became closer as friends, I began to realize that Lisa indeed had a number of interesting, if not rather *startling* qualities. For instance, there were times where, during our discussions, Lisa could seem to sense things about me that I wouldn't actually ever say, and would later divulge them. In other instances, one of us would curiously seem to grasp onto things the other had been thinking and say them aloud, as though we could literally read each other's minds; something I had never experienced to any frequent degree with another sole individual. And on several other occasions, I would find myself suddenly thinking of Lisa; only to find that she was calling me at the very instant I had reached for my phone to do the same. We eventually began to acknowledge that this unique connection existed between us—despite whatever the source for this may have been. Such friendships are seldom found in life, and thus ours became a friendship of the very best variety, as well as one I could rely on during such strange instances as my predicament at Reynolds Mansion on the evening of Tuesday, September 18, 2012.

Initially, when I asked Lisa to make the two-hour drive down to Asheville for the evening, she had been hesitant; not only because of the long travel time on a week night, but also because of the actual potential that something might indeed happen during the séance I was planning.

"Bottom line," she told me over the phone earlier that afternoon, "I don't want to get creeped out and then have to drive all the way back to Highlands in the dark by myself." I told her I understood completely, and as usual, tried to disguise my disappointment, though I have found with time that this is impossible to do with Lisa.

"Micah, don't get angry with me."

"I'm not, you know better than that."

"Yes," she added, "but you *are* getting testy."

"Absolutely not," I argued. She was right, though. Hence, realizing I had taken too much of her time already, I cheerfully told her not to be concerned, and that I nonetheless hoped she might be able to visit Reynolds Mansion another day.

To my utter surprise, later that afternoon I received another call from her, stating that she had changed her mind. She didn't explain why, or what had motivated her, but assured me that she would be leaving work a bit early so she could be in Asheville and on hand, ready to lend her skill as a photographer to assist with documenting our psychic experiment. Had our séance been planned for any of the previous dates I had tried to arrange, Lisa's presence would never have even been a consideration; and yet, somehow, the old adage stating that all things happen how they do, and *when* they do, for a reason had proven true yet again, and in the most delightful manner I could presently imagine.

❖   ❖   ❖

Prior to our séance that evening, Lisa joined me for a visit to the Reynolds family plot in Riverside Cemetery, one of several historic locations in Asheville. There we walked together through the crisp autumn air, hoping the storm clouds that had centered themselves over town this evening might hold off for just long enough to allow us a visit with the former residents of Reynolds Mansion. Passing the graves of literary names the likes of O. Henry and Thomas Wolfe, as well as Civil War governor Zebulon Vance, we made our way up the hill toward the first site where members of the Reynolds family were laid to rest.

"I'm surprised you would want to come with me to a place like this," I said.

"Why not?" Lisa asked. "I think this is a fabulous place, and graveyards are interesting. It's very quiet here, and very still. I can see why you enjoy it so much."

"Well that, and I also figured it might be good luck to visit the graves of some of the people we hope to reach out to later tonight," I told her. As we made our way along the hillside, the graves of Senator Robert Rice Reynolds, and that of his son, came into view. We stopped by this first section of the Reynolds family gravestones and lingered for some time, before we finally trudged off down the hill a bit further, toward the site where Daniel Reynolds, his wife, and the mysterious Annie Lee Reynolds were buried.

"Micah, what do you think is really going to happen tonight?" Lisa asked.

"Damned if I know," I admitted. "Just between us, I'm not certain how much likelihood there is of us actually making any contact with a spirit. But who knows, we might learn something nonetheless."

Lisa remained silent for a moment. "And what about other ghosts? What if we spoke to someone other than one of the Reynolds spirits?"

"Well, there are the stories about embalming that took place on the property. If any spirits were to actually make themselves known to us, I imagine they might be likely candidates too."

"But that's not really what I meant," Lisa said. "I was thinking, what if somebody that one of us had known was to come through?"

"Like who? Did you have anyone in mind?"

"Yes, maybe."

I stopped long enough to study Lisa's expression, which was bright and positive, as she normally is, though I could sense something different that had come over her entirely... something I had never felt before when we were together.

"Who is it?" I asked.

"I had secretly hoped that I might hear from my father, or perhaps my brother." Indeed, Lisa had lost two family members over the last several years. Perhaps her reasons for changing her mind and wanting to join were now becoming clear.

"Well maybe so," I started to say.

"Those aren't my only reasons for coming down though," she added. "You know I'm interested in this sort of stuff, too. But most of all, I just felt like I was supposed to be here."

"Oh yeah?"

"Yes," she said. "I felt like you might need me."

"Well you do have a sense for those sorts of things," I said, a bit surprised by Lisa's sudden admission. "Let's hope you're right." Her brown eyes widened, and she smiled at me as I spoke, withdrawing her camera and pulling a lock of hair behind her ear as she turned and knelt by the grave of Annie Lee Reynolds. While I watched her take a photo, the first droplets of cold rain finally began to fall from the threatening sky overhead, striking the surface of the tombstones before us and signaling our departure for what would be our final destination of the evening.

"Can you get the heavy draperies and close them?" Marti asked, motioning to Matt, who was setting up audio equipment we had piled onto the bed in guestroom Lila. "That's just in case we have guests walking by the windows outside on the porch," she explained, as Lisa laughed in agreement with Marti's assessment of the situation.

"That's right, we don't want to scare the other guests with our occult interests," I said in jest, although judging from the weather this evening, it was unlikely that anyone would care to be outside on such a night. Heavy clouds and fog had rested over Asheville for the duration of the afternoon, and as the early evening had crept closer, rain and wind had begun to ensue.

Once Matt had pulled the drapes, Marti dimmed the lights to near-darkness, and we began to take our seats around a small oak table Billy had provided for us before he left for the evening. Lisa pulled her chair in close to mine on the left, positioning herself just between Marti and I to provide the best photographic advantage. Matt was sitting directly to my right, and Chris completed the circle by sitting across from me. A hush began to fall over the room, and we soon felt the silence of the surrounding darkness begin to envelope us.

"Chris," I said, looking across at my producer, whose eyes still betrayed a modicum of disbelief. "*Now* we get serious."

"I'm always serious," he whispered, somewhat chastened.

"By the way," Marti interjected. "I'm not sure that this will mean anything, but I made it a point to wear this tonight." She moved her right hand toward the center of the table, revealing a small golden ring she wore that encased a dark red stone. "I had a friend that passed away about a year ago who left me some jewelry. So I wore her ring."

"What was her name?" I asked.

"Her name was Patty."

"Well perhaps Patty's good luck will be here with us tonight," I offered hopefully. I wondered now if Lisa were the only one with secret hopes that a friend or loved one might come into our otherworldly conversation this evening.

"And now, let's begin."

Before undertaking our séance, I felt that it would be best to carry out one tradition common among many spiritualists, which involves helping construct what could be likened to a psychic "egg of protection" around each participant. I asked my company to begin by placing their feet flat against the floor, and advised that they may choose to remove their shoes if this aided their comfort. I also recommended that we close our eyes, if this helped with visualizing the protective barrier we would hope to build around each individual in the room.

"Keep your legs uncrossed, and your backs straight. And finally, we'll place our hands on the table, palms facing down with the tips of your thumbs touching. By allowing the tips of our little fingers to touch, we will create a circle, in which we are all connected with each other." Marti, being the most petite among us, had mild difficulty extending her digits widely enough to join the rest, but we were nonetheless able to manage a nice, uniform circle between the hands of our participants, while Miss Northrup remained beside me, quietly documenting our experiment with photographs.

"Our hands together like this look like an Iron Cross," Chris said abruptly, referencing the German military decoration for bravery, which first began to see use around 1813. "Are you sure this isn't going to be a Nazi occult ritual?"

"There may be a bit of *Vril* involved," I said with a chuckle, and then advised that we all begin to focus on the events at hand.

"We'll begin by breathing very deeply," I began. "Imagine the energy of the Earth rising up through the ground, and passing through the floors in this old building. It passes through the carpet, and into your legs, rising up through your body. The Earth has a very strong energy to it, and I want you to equate this with whomever you pray to, or what you draw your power from: God, or perhaps the essence of cosmic universal love. Now feel that energy coming up through the ground, up into you, and enveloping you and your spirit. Imagine a color—I prefer to use white, as it is a color often associated with goodness—and imagine that color enveloping you, moving outward from within as though encasing you in a protective egg." Taking a moment to glance over my left shoulder, I could see that Lisa's eyes were closed, and that she had been going through this protective procedure with us; I had hoped she would, in fact, particularly because of her apparent aptitude for the psychic arts.

"This applies to you too, of course," I said to her softly.

I continued, asking my company to feel this protective barrier of light surrounding their entire bodies, and extending outward into the room, so that they were surrounded by it on all sides by several inches. "This will form a cosmic egg, so to speak, that negativity or evil may never crack. Imagine this light surrounding you and *protecting* you like a hard shell, and know that this energy barrier you have put up around yourself will protect you from any adversity. You are safe, you are happy, and you are *home*, here at Reynolds Mansion tonight, and for the duration of this psychic experiment.

"During this experience we will seek to communicate with those who are no longer among the living. There are two names that I wish to divulge specifically, with hope that one of these individuals may make his or her presence known to us: The first is Daniel Reynolds. We are in Daniel's former chamber this very evening, as we conduct this séance. The former master of the home, and the man who built this residence in which, at least for the evening, we act as residents together. We would like to see if

Daniel might come across the barrier between worlds, and indicate his presence through the tappings and turnings of this table.

"Or perhaps there is another: there is a young girl that is occasionally seen here, and we believe that she may be Annie Lee Reynolds. If Annie Lee or Daniel were present here, we would wish for them to feel comfortable enough to come through and make their presence known, and to pass along information to us if they can. The way that this information will be passed along through the turnings of the table will be simple: all that we need is for this table to slightly turn in one direction or another. To tip up on two legs will indicate a *yes,* while a no will be indicated by the absence of any activity.

"And with that," I finally said, having divulged our instructions for the first portion of the experiment, "we will begin."

Breathing deeply and allowing a moment of silence, I quickly glanced around at the others, noticing that every one in my company still had their eyes closed, as though entranced by the proceedings taking place thus far. By all indications, I had succeeded within a few short minutes at creating a quiet, meditative, and perhaps even a *hypnotic* environment, in which the subtle thoughts and influences of each person might project into the environment and become amplified.

"I would like to ask first if there are any here with us this evening that would wish to make their presence known. If so, please indicate *yes* in the described method, by tilting one end of the table for us."

I then turned my attention from the hidden residents among us for the next few moments, and addressed the participants of our séance. "While we conduct this experiment, I want all of you to please keep your mind open to any sudden images or thoughts that may come to mind, especially those which seem to appear very suddenly, or from nowhere. You may want to share those, because often it is the case in these instances that strange messages do tend to be received. It's very difficult at times to discern between a psychic message and what is perceived merely as a thought. But in this instance you will hopefully be able to recognize a very clear, defined sort of thought; one that may just leap to mind, often very obscure or random in nature. If that should happen, you may want to share it with the rest of us during the proceedings tonight."

I allowed for a few moments of silence, and then restated my intentions to attempt to establish contact with one of the former members of the Reynolds home. "It is said by many that there is a man that enters this room, who is particularly unhappy about the door behind us always remaining closed and locked. I've made certain that it is unlocked for the duration of our time here tonight, but I wonder, is this Daniel Reynolds, and if so, Daniel are you here present with us tonight? Again, if a spirit is present, you may indicate your presence through the movement of this table."

I allowed several more moments of silence at this point, where we all relaxed our bodies, and waited to see if any movement may occur that would indicate a presence in the room with us aside from one of the known members of our company. I then repeated the questions, but despite the careful construction of a "psychic" environment, the oak table that Billy had provided us with for the experiment, despite its small size, was also thick and heavy, and would not seem to budge. Ideally, furniture fitted for use in table turning experiments should feature a round tabletop, three legs, and if possible, should be constructed entirely of wood. Although our table was indeed built of thick oak, it featured a square surface, and had been fitted with four legs. A smaller, round table with the

221

preferred number of legs had remained against the wall in an adjacent room; while I had initially hoped to use this one in our experiment, Billy had felt that a flaw in the table's surface might cause it to be too fragile for our purposes. Thus, even with the help of human hands, it seemed that the table we were provided had simply been too sturdy to be affected by any subtleties stemming from the spirit realm.

"I fear that our table may be too large," I said after a few more attempts at establishing contact in this way. Turning to Marti, I asked how she might feel about acting as our "medium" for the next phase of the experiment.

"I don't have to speak in tongues or anything, do I?" she asked cautiously.

"Not at all," I assured her. "You only need to hold this pendulum between your thumb and forefinger. That's all."

Marti took the pendulum in her hand, and held the string so that the weighted end might dangle close to the surface of the table. "Alright, perfect," I said, telling Marti that if her arm began to get tired from holding the pendulum suspended over the table in this way, that she could rest her elbow against the edge nearest to her. "Let's go ahead and assume that a simple, forward and backward motion will indicate *yes* in this instance, and if we see a circular motion, that will mean *no*. And now Marti, perhaps one of the most psychic among us, is going to act as our medium."

Before we began, I allowed Marti a moment to get comfortable in her position, and then asked her to simply hold the pendulum while I asked it to show us a clear circular motion to indicate "no," as well as a back and forward movement to indicate a clear "yes." Very quickly in both instances, the pendulum began to move in the prescribed manner, although we found that in

Marti's case, the movements were often very small. Therefore, at times it could be difficult to discern precisely whether the motion we were seeing was a yes or a no response.

"Lets see if we can gather any information like this," I said once we were finished preparing our methods for pendulum reading. "This time I would like to begin by asking, is there is a young spirit, perhaps a young girl, somewhere here at Reynolds Mansion?" The pendulum began swinging first with a very small, ambiguous movement, before it eventually started to round itself into an elliptical pattern.

"Looks like a no," I commented, though perhaps a bit too soon; almost in coincidence with my spoken observation, the pendulum had begun to change its movement to reflect a positive response.

"Or is it a yes?" I said, now a bit puzzled. Turning to Lisa, I asked her, serving as our objective observer, whether she felt the pendulum had been indicating a positive or negative response, as it appeared from her vantage. As I looked toward her, I watched Lisa's eyebrows begin to rise, a perplexed expression now crossing her face.

"It stopped!" She whispered.

"It *stopped?*" I said. Indeed, the pendulum had stopped moving altogether.

"Am I causing this?" Marti said, a bit frustrated. "I mean, I think I'm holding my hand completely still, that's what I'm supposed to do, right?"

"Absolutely right," I assured her.

"Maybe you should start by asking something more general," Chris said. "Start by simply asking if there is a spirit, and then progress from there."

"Very well," I agreed. "Let's begin now by asking, simply, if there is a spirit here at Reynolds Mansion, that might like to come through and communicate with us here tonight? If you are present, we are looking to see if there is a spirit present at Reynolds Mansion that would be willing to communicate with us." Again, we gave the pendulum time to issue a discernable movement; to my surprise, the movement of the pendulum this time had been quite clear.

"It looks like a *no!*" I exclaimed. "So are there *no spirits* at Reynolds Mansion?" Were we dealing with a shy ghost, or merely none at all? Or perhaps had Marti's own inner reservations about contacting the spirit realm been influencing the movement of the pendulum?

"Micah, let's suppose for just a moment that the movement of the pendulum actually *were* the result of some spirit's influence," Chris said, breaking from his typical skeptical tendencies. "Wouldn't it be odd that we would be asking whether a spirit were present with us, and the response should be *no?* We would be dealing with a lying ghost!" Indeed, Chris's observation, even as a thought experiment, mirrored my own logic; if we were even to suppose that a spirit's presence were capable of influencing the outcome of our questions during the séance, we might assume that any activity at all would indicate some variety of presence in our midst... but what, precisely, might it be? I decided I would ask for clarification.

"My next question is whether a spirit, here present, is in any way controlling the movement of the pendulum now. Are you associated with Reynolds Mansion?" Again, the swinging of the pendulum began to issue a *yes*, but then seemed to change its mind again after several moments. Perhaps I had neglected to designate a

224

clear response that would indicate "maybe" in the event that we encountered a shy or playful spirit presence.

"I'm a bit confused," I said with a chuckle, "because I'm getting both responses. So in other words, there *may* be someone associated with Reynolds Mansion who is influencing the movement of the pendulum, but that there is no spirit here who is an actual resident at Reynolds Mansion." I had to laugh at the situation, and after thinking about the circumstances for a moment, I then had an interesting image come to mind; I recalled the psychic that visited the mansion, Kristy Robinett, saying that the spirit of a young girl had approached her, and claimed that she had been embalmed here. Indeed, it had seemed to be a rather odd, if not a slightly grisly remark at the time, even for a ghost to be making. Later, of course, it was revealed to Billy that not only had Nat Augustus Reynolds been the operator of a funeral home, but he had also used a building on the property directly adjacent to the mansion for embalming corpses that were being prepared for funerals. What if there were spirits here that hadn't been associated with the Reynolds family after all?

"Is there a spirit here who was *never* a resident at Reynolds Mansion?" I asked. Again, we allowed a long silence as we waited to see how the movement of the pendulum would respond.

"No," Chris said quietly, as we watched the small weight at the end of the string spin in a slight circle. By now, we were beginning to feel that the pendulum and its responses might have been a bit too erratic, if not altogether difficult to discern at times.

"There is always one final option," I said, looking over my right shoulder toward the bed where our equipment was resting.

"The Ouija board," Marti said, a bit of stress in her voice becoming apparent. Prior to our experiment, Marti had, like my mother, expressed definite concern about the use of Ouija boards during our psychic experiment. As it turns out, she and her mother had experimented with one together several years ago, and much like my own mother's story, both had been badly frightened by the information the device seemed capable of relating to them. She had chosen, however, not to elaborate on the specifics of the incident.

"We can thank Billy," I joked, "for not getting the nice, small table that I wanted."

"Well how bad is the crack in that three legged table?" Chris asked.

Marti shook her head. "I'm afraid Billy doesn't want us to use it."

"Bad enough, it seems." I tried to remain hopeful. "Although I really had wanted to use *that* table."

Lisa leaned in close. "If you use that Ouija board, your mom is probably going to disown you," she whispered. Then she nudged me with her elbow. "But you probably should use it anyway." I had been surprised by this remark, and glancing up at her, I was met with a playful, if not mischievous smile from the brown-eyed beauty.

"The Ouija?" I said, surprised. She nodded.

"But if you use that Oujia board," Chris began, "Then Marti is going to recuse herself from the rest of us, and you're going to have to come in and join us, Lisa!"

"Well, can we try something else before you do that?" Marti asked hopefully.

"We'll need to establish a more clear way of getting clear yes and no answers using the pendulum if we do," I remarked. "After all, our spirits seem to be quite the tricksters this evening."

"Should you give it a try?" Marti asked.

"As the leader of the séance, I had preferred not to actually hold the pendulum myself. If I were to hold the pendulum, I know Chris would be well equipped to lead with questions, and I would need him to do so to maintain some degree of objectivity.

"Wait," Lisa said. "Let me try."

"But I thought you didn't want to…" I began to say, as Lisa took the pendulum from my hands. Indeed, prior to our arrival at Reynolds Mansion, Lisa had stated she felt more comfortable merely observing and taking photos during our séance.

"I just have a feeling," she said. I handed the pendulum to Lisa, and allowed her to grasp the length of cord attached to the weight, assuming the position with her elbow resting gently toward the edge of the table nearest her. Almost immediately, the lights in the large chandelier hanging above us began to flicker violently. Marti and I looked at one another, and then up at the lights, which were still coming and going as though the power were going out.

"Marti, are the lights doing something bizarre?" I asked. Matt and Chris were both looking at me, each of them carrying a troubled expression, but despite the curious electrical phenomena occurring over our heads, I decided to ignore it and proceed.

"Alright, we've now passed the pendulum along to Miss Lisa Northrup," I said aloud, so that the events as they happened could be noted using the recording equipment behind me. And again, just as surely as I spoke Lisa's name in conjunction with her holding the pendulum, the lights resumed their erratic flashing; in this instance, the chandelier above us went out completely for a few seconds, almost prompting me to think we had lost electrical power for at least a few moments.

"The lights are beginning to do some strange things," I said again, "in coincidence with Lisa taking the pendulum, I should note." We allowed the pendulum to steady itself, and proceeded again with the customary designations of "yes" and "no"; in this instance, each of the responses yielded very clearly, while the strange, erratic electrical activity continued overhead. As a more prosaic explanation for the interference, Marti and I supposed that there might be something going on in the room directly above us, where there had been a couple staying on the evening in question. However, we would not learn the true extent of the odd disturbances that coincided with Lisa Northrup's choice to enter our séance until much later.

"Again, I would now like to ask if there is a spirit present that would be willing to communicate with us. A simple yes or no response will help us determine this." I watched the pendulum's movement, and this time we began to see a clear "yes" emanating from the side-to-side movement of the pendulum. As I asked for clarification of this from the others seated around the table, I began to notice that the movement had almost come to a pause, and then stopped altogether. Throughout the several seconds of motion we had observed, the lights above us had continued to flicker rather violently, which had become distracting to Marti.

"With the lights, I'm wondering it that's people going upstairs," Marti said, "or maybe moving around in the room above us."

"Does that happen often?" I asked.

"I don't know," she admitted, "because I'm not usually here in the evenings. I'll have to ask Billy."

"Was this recently installed?" I asked, pointing to the chandelier. Marti told me that it wasn't.

At this point, I feel that I should depart briefly from the narrative of events unfolding during our séance, only to note that

Marti had indeed been very troubled by the electrical interference we had witnessed; enough that she decided to follow up with Billy about it later that evening, once the rest of us left the mansion. Though we hadn't known it at the time, our host, who had excused himself due to work that prevented him from joining us, had returned from dinner by the time our séance was underway, and had been in the library beside us working, just on the other side of the wall nearest to Lisa and Marti. In addition to witnessing the strange electrical interference, Billy was alarmed by the fact that the motor in the fish tank, which rested by the wall our two rooms shared, had begun to make a strange noise, as though it were losing power. Billy told Marti that it had never done this before, nor has it seemed to experience any problems since, though he described the noise as sounding like the motor "had been losing power." After investigating the noise, he found no reason for the disturbance, noting that this also coincided with the flickering lights overhead. Returning to his desk, Billy resumed his work, only to find within a few moments that his computer had shut off, although power had never actually been lost at any time (as I might have incorrectly guessed, based on the way the lights behaved at their very worst).

"What were you all doing in there?" Billy asked Marti.

"All I know is that the lights began to come and go right at the moment Micah handed the pendulum to Lisa Northrup," Marti told him. She then asked him about the situation with the lights, and whether that happened often in the evenings. As she recapped her conversation with Billy to me the following day, Marti explained that Billy reminded her how the electrical wiring had been redone entirely once the house had been purchased. He also stated firmly that, after spending almost every evening at the mansion since he and Michael had opened to the public, there had *never* been problems with lighting like what he witnessed in Reynolds Mansion the night of our séance.

❖   ❖   ❖

After continuing a while longer with the pendulum, we decided finally that we would try changing our method of exchange with the spirit realm, so as to make the best use of our available time.

"There's always the Ouija board," I said again, drawing a mixed response from the others in the room.

"I don't…" Marti began, trailing off into uneasy laughter. Lisa's large eyes glared at me, though she was less verbal about her hesitation than Marti.

"Ladies, if you don't feel comfortable with the Ouija," I said, looking over at Matt and Chris, "then we paranormalists can take the helm here on this one.

"Now I have never utilized a Ouija board before," I explained. "And you have to keep in mind that, just as with many other things, these can be used potentially for divination. But there's always that negative potential that exists, which is why I asked each of you to build up that protective barrier of white light in your minds before we began. I do want everyone to be comfortable with the proceedings, more than anything."

I continued trying to quell everyone's fears as I explained more about the process underlying the use of Ouija boards. "You have to keep in mind also that the popular literature, and what we see in films, indicates that these things are terrible, and that they bring demons into the world. That is very seldom what does actually happen, and we can't discount the number of positive experiences people have had with the things just as well, especially when they are used responsibly."

I removed the Ouija board from its packaging, the very same which its owner had mailed it to us in, and brought it over to our table. Then, removing a small metal cross from my breast pocket, I placed it on top of the planchette, both as a measure of protection, but also to accentuate the directional capacity of the device we would use to point to individual letters on the surface of the Ouija board.

"Gentlemen," I began, "let's undertake something now that I'd hoped we would not have to do tonight."

"Wait," Marti interrupted. "We're getting close to the end of the time we've been allowed for this evening. Would you prefer to try this final experiment in Annie Lee's room on the third floor?"

"Absolutely," Chris interjected.

"Okay, yes," I said in agreement. "It might be good to try our luck in another part of the house. Why don't we head upstairs?" Surely, while our results in guestroom Lila had been very interesting, the odd disturbances we were noticing may not have had to do entirely with anything emanating from the house. Perhaps, if Annie Lee Reynolds really had anything to do with the nature of the haunting at Reynolds Mansion, we might fare better at garnering insight in the location here that she had been most familiar with.

❖　❖　❖

My company and I took what little equipment we were using and began our ascent toward the third floor, with Matt bundling our recording equipment beneath each arm, and Chris heaving the large oak table Billy had allowed us to use back up the stairs to its location on the second floor. We moved silently along, carrying out our work so that none of the occupants in guest rooms we passed might be disturbed. Finally, we reached the top of the stairs, and entering Maggie's Room, the former chamber of Annie Lee Reynolds, I allowed everyone to pass before closing and locking the door behind us.

This, our final destination, had essentially served as my introduction to the odd occurrences here at Reynolds Mansion, after my first sleepless night lying on the bed adjacent to where we now were placing recording equipment, laptop computers, and a small table where the Ouija board would rest throughout this portion of our experiment. Once we finished setting up all our belongings, I joined Matt and Chris at the table in the center of the room, and positioned the planchette near the middle of the Ouija board.

"Marti, is there a portrait of Annie Lee that we could borrow from one of the walls?" She nodded in agreement, and I asked if she would go fetch it for us.

"Are your hands on the board?" Chris asked. "I've never really used one of these before."

"Good question," I said. "We just want to keep our fingers lightly touching the planchette, which is this little moving piece. As we ask questions, it will begin to move, and it will move from letter to letter, which will help us to learn what any spirit presences may hope to convey to us tonight.

"So I'd like to begin by again stating that we wish to bathe ourselves, all here present, in that protective light." I paused briefly. "In cosmic love, truly," I added for good measure, drawing a few smiles from my uneasy associates. "The light of goodness, and the light of protection, so that no wickedness, and no evil, shall enter the bubble of goodness that surrounds the five of us. We are all protected by the power of earth, and by the power of the cosmos."

Again I paused, and looking up, met halfway with Lisa in mid-gaze. "By the power of *God*," I added, allowing the weight of these words to sink in among my company before returning my attention to the table again.

"And now, we will begin by asking our questions. At this point, here in the room of Annie Lee Reynolds… this was your room in life, and if you are here present, I would like to invite you to indicate your presence through the movement of the planchette across the surface of the Ouija board." After several moments, the planchette began to drift slowly, though aimlessly, never pausing before any particular letter. For good measure, I decided to ask that the planchette stop moving for a moment, so as to identify the movement as being some variety of intentional action; either on part of Matt, Chris, and I, or through the influence of some external force. As requested, the object stopped moving, and we again resumed our questions, after which the planchette now remained still for several long minutes.

"My back is killing me," Chris finally said. Indeed, the posture one must maintain with the movement of the planchette ideally has one keeping their fingers only lightly poised along the sides of the small pointing tool, and one's elbows raised above the surface of the table, to grant freedom of movement as the planchette begins to make its way across the surface of the board. I advised Chris to rest a few moments, and that Matt and I would continue in the meantime.

"Let's try it with just you and I, Matt. Again, the gentle movement of the planchette will indicate if there may be a presence here in this room with us; thus, I will ask again if we are joined in this room by a former occupant of Reynolds Mansion?"

Almost immediately, the planchette began to move, and we watched as the tip of the device glided toward the right end of the board, coming to rest before a single letter, then resuming its curious pause.

"The letter *I*," I said aloud. "What is the significance of that letter?"

"Maybe you can now ask questions that are yes or no answers," Marti suggested.

"Matt, let's try to learn more about the significance of that letter." We began to repeat our questioning again, intended to reveal the presence of any spirit in our midst, this time indicated through the movement of the planchette either to the positions of "yes" or "no" near the top of the board. This lasted for several more minutes, but the planchette curiously maintained its position over the letter "I". I had wondered if this could have been the rough equivalent of the old English term "aye," meant to indicate yes; or perhaps it had been a Roman numeral for the number one that was intended; and yet, there were clearly labeled numbers spanning the base of the board, as well as both yes and no responses oriented near the top. If there had been any significance to this particular letter being revealed at all, I wondered also if it could have been intended for use as a subject pronoun, perhaps indicating something along the lines of a very simple, "I am here!"

By now, my party and I had been drawing very near to the end of the time our host had allotted for our psychic experiment. "It seems we have managed to glean two bits of information from our spirit company tonight: one, they are telling us there are *no spirits* at Reynolds Mansion, and two, that they said 'I'. Very curious."

Chris made a rather oblique reference to our "spirit" being that of a deceased actor, while Lisa and Marti exchanged perplexed looks and giggles. However, before we resolved our séance, I decided to try one final, very brief experiment.

"Are there any books in this room?"

"Yes," Marti said. "There are these old ones I donated to Billy," she said, bringing to my attention a set of elderly volumes stacked on the desk behind Matt where he had positioned our audio equipment.

"Perfect," I said. "These are going to be most useful for us, because we're going to use these books for our final experiment." I began to disperse the stack of old books throughout the room, handing one to each person, and then collecting an old leather-bound volume of Victor Hugo's collected works for myself.

"Now, this is a very simple experiment, involving what is known as *bibliomancy*. It essentially means to discern information supernaturally by interpreting a randomly chosen passage from a book. All you need to do is open your book to any random page, and to conclude this evening's experiments, I'll have each of your read the first line that your eyes fall upon."

As I spoke, most everyone had been paying attention to my instructions, save only Lisa, who was already bent over her open volume, looking at the open pages of her book.

"Lisa," I advised, "the aim of this experiment is not to *read* the book I've handed you!" We all began to laugh.

"But you should see what the line I turned to says!" She fired back at me. Drawing near, she pointed to the first line she had spotted, which read, *"There may be nothing in it for you!"*

"That's weird," she said, laughing. It seemed that the supernatural forces in our midst were intent on playing the trickster role to the very end.

"Alright, well I think that's enough practice. Let's try this officially," I began again. "I want each of you to take the book I've handed you, and to turn to any random page. Whatever single place on the page your eyes first may fall, read that sentence, and we're going to see if we can glean any kind of information by doing so. Alright, now open your books."

Each of us opened the book we had received, and I elected to read my passage first, which appeared to be an excerpt from Hugo's *Ninety Three*, that read as follows: *"There is an hour of the day which may be called noiseless: it is the serene hour of early evening. It was about him now. He enjoyed it."*

"Matthew," I asked, indicating for him to share his sentence. In his typical raspy tone, Matt shared his passage, which simply read, *"'I don't see how you can do anything else,' he declared."*

"Marti?"

"That had been a wonderful day," she replied.

"It had indeed," I added. "Chris?"

"Some of the stories permitted a common sense explanation," he read, allowing his gaze to join with mine. Always the skeptic, his had

been perhaps the most fitting thus far. I couldn't fight back a smile, and Matt, Lisa and Marti burst out laughing at the utter irony.

"Funny, coming from you Chris," Marti added.

"Indeed," I said, "And finally, Lisa."

Finer, perhaps, than any Shakespearian leading lady, Lisa declaimed her passage to the rest of us, lifting her words like the dancing wing beats of a fluttering moth against the stale air of the room.

"*The artist dipped his brush again.*" She smiled.

"How beautiful," I whispered. "And thus endeth our séance." It was a fine ending indeed; and for the record, it seemed a very fitting way to conclude, for the moment, our pursuit of the mysteries at hand—despite whatever secrets they might have yielded otherwise—and thus allow this desirous and spirited young artist to find a new place to dip his brush, just as the lady before me had so wisely suggested. Throughout the course of the night, we never managed to find conclusive evidence of our ghosts; but in a sense, we had been given something far more valuable instead: a warm and very memorable evening, spent with the best company one could imagine, and one that had been rife with synchronicity and strange phenomena nonetheless.

In my estimation, the brush strokes of our minds had decorated this evening's canvas with an unusual and colorful portrait, indeed. It was a rare sort of masterpiece we had created together, and one that few will ever manage to find at even the finest gallery or auction.

Afterword

"YOU KNOW MICAH, I THINK YOU AND I OUGHT TO CONSIDER writing a cookbook next, once your book on Reynolds Mansion is done." Billy chuckled at his own proposition. "But seriously, I think it would be a good idea."

"Oh you know me," I said in agreement. "I'd hardly be opposed to much of anything, so long as it involves this place."

"So what do you think about Reynolds Mansion and its ghosts now? You aren't throwing in the towel on your hope for finding them yet, are you?"

"I wouldn't say I'm giving up," I told him. "I just think it has more to do with there simply being an odd feeling of closure now. It's almost as if, supposing that there may really be spirits of some kind here, they've given me only the slightest glimpse of themselves. It's like they want to say, *yes, here we are… but now that you know, that's all you get.*"

"So you've still never seen one?" Billy asked.

"No, and in a way, I'm not sure they want me to see them. In fact, I'm not entirely certain I can, in good faith, refer to them as being 'they' at all!"

Billy looked perplexed, as he poured more tea over the ice in the bottom of his tumbler. "Well what in the world is that supposed to mean?"

"I'll tell you this," I said, still grasping for words. "My experiences here at this mansion have almost entirely changed my perception of what a 'ghost' may or may not be. I think that, as I entered this environment, I was attached to the same old stereotype that so many latch onto: ghosts are spirits of the dead, and they have unfinished business. But having a place like this to come and visit—it's not just a sense of having a home away from home; it's like having a *laboratory*—and I feel like I've managed to come here, observe the place, hear its stories, and learn its history. Most of all, I've had time to *think*. And now, I'm not sure that I can rest all my cards, in good faith, on the simple notion that people just die, and then ghosts sometimes stick around a place afterward.

"Think about it," I continued. "Although there have been guests who have all but tried to make up stories about the place having sadness, or maybe a negative energy of some kind that haunts the place, in truth I can't deny this being one of the happiest, most comfortable, and maybe just one of the *best* places on Earth. It seems like there couldn't be a reason why restless spirits would need to stick around if they had lived here."

"Unless maybe they just loved it too much to ever leave," Billy offered. "Although I do see what you're saying, you have to admit, if there was one place a ghost might ever want to come back and visit, it would have to be here."

"Yes, you're right," I said. "In fact, I could hardly imagine a better place for spirits to want to make as a regular retreat; whether they be alive, dead, or something else altogether."

By now it was getting late, and I had a long drive ahead of me, so I bid my host farewell, once again, and thanked him for the tea, trail mix, and of course, the conversation that was always something one can find at this curious old country home. On my way toward the back door, from which it had become customary that I would use when making my exits, I turned once again, peering down the hallway toward the library, just in case there might be anyone waiting; perhaps a young lady, sporting some long, fancy dress of decades past, as she made her way back up the stairs toward her chamber.

"Billy, I think there are things about Reynolds Mansion that I'm just not supposed to ever know," I concluded. "Maybe nobody is supposed to ever know about them. Whether it's silver buried somewhere on the property, or a secret kept in a journal or other document hidden away in a tunnel or passage—whatever it is, I think that part of what makes this place special is that those secrets remain kept from us, *forever*. For me, I know they keep me guessing, and they keep me wanting to come back, whether or not they're something I'll ever find."

"Well I suppose that's good, in a way," my host added. "After all, if my home manages to have that same appeal with all the folks that visit here, I know I'll be in business for a long time to come!" We both laughed at Billy's hopeful prediction, and shook hands once more before I descended the stairs entering the garden, which even in the early fall remained beautiful, new looking, and full of life.

"Come back again soon," Billy called after me. "You've still got to give your parents a tour some time, and bring Lisa back so she can photograph the guest rooms on the second floor!"

"Don't worry, I'll make a point of it," I said with a wave.

I made my way along that familiar brick path, and as I passed beneath the old swaying pine trees in the back yard, I felt the gravel begin to crunch beneath my feet as that autumn breeze carried along the familiar scent of summer's end. For many, this is a colorful, invigorating time of year; but it is also a time when beautiful things recoil away from the cold, and return into the recesses of the soft earth to await the warmth of spring. It is a time for closure, and perhaps also a time for reflection.

Reflection is a fine pastime to adopt at a place such as this, regardless of the season or time of day. It is a place for comfort, but it is also a place for secrets. It is a place for friends, but also a place for silence. It is a place that is inviting in every way, but also one that calls out to you at night, and will keep the restless heart and mind awake with its secrets.

"Yes," I said, turning to look back at her one more time, stopping and taking in the daylight that illuminated the long, well-traveled path between us.

"I'll be back again."

Bibliography

Belanger, Jeff. *The World's Most Haunted Places, Revised Edition.* New Page Books, 2011.

"Folk Art Center Celebrates Its 70th Anniversary in Asheville, NC." http://www.carolinaarts.com/600folkart.html

Jung, Carl Gustav. *The Red Book (Liber Novus).* Translated by Mark Kyburz, John Peck and Sodu Shamdasani. Philemon Series & W.W. Norton & Co. 2009.

Kim, Ashida. *Secrets of the Ninja.* Citadel, 2001.

McLean, Joseph. *The Hope Diamond: Evalyn Walsh McClean and the Captivating Mystery of the World's Most Alluring Jewel.* Providence House Publishers. Franklin, Tennessee. 2011.

Nesbitt, A. William. "History of Early Settlement and Land Use on the Bent Creek Experimental Forest, Buncombe County, N.C." Appalachian Forest Experiment Station, Asheville, North Carolina. December 10, 1941

Pleasants, Julian. *Buncombe Bob: The Life and Times of Robert Rice Reynolds.* University of North Carolina Press, 2000.

Pye, Michael and Kirsten Daley. *Ghosts, Spirits, and Hauntings: Am I Being Haunted?* New Page Books, 2011.

Reynolds Mansion Records with the Department of the Interior: https://docs.google.com/viewer?a=v&q=cache:7N2lyEVVp0UJ:w ww.hpo.ncdcr.gov/nr/BN0176.pdf+&hl=en&gl=us&pid=bl&srci d=ADGEESiC5ETr2JarHy9dyITWu-aeMUDktK6sQXVxUU2 cda66KklC2TE_-nbWaPhPNQ4kXh-tC2--lG0HGE88LC4uy_N0 DHBjhysIz5DQ_62sMWG8zTyOGk4Phmyhuz9ZXPw-7IBKe 7Zy&sig=AHIEtbT6D2V8wf_meHhpMB1tBNXpPu2Pfw&pli=1

Runnels, Moses Thurston. *A Genealogy of Runnels and Reynolds Families in America.* A. Mudge and Son, 1873. http://archive.org/ stream/genealogyofrunne00runn#page/n3/mode/2up.

"'Showman' Bob Reynolds Puts Eccentric New Fiancée in Washington Spotlight." *The Pittsburgh Press,* Sep 14, 1941. http://news.google.com/newspapers?id=PVIbAAAAIBAJ&sjid=c 0wEAAAAIBAJ&pg=3319,1414092&dq=mclean+reynolds+suicid e&hl=en

Surprise, Kirby. *Synchronicity: The Art of Coincidence, Choice, and Unlocking Your Mind.*

The Official Reference Book of the Press Club of Chicago, 1922.http://books.google.com/books?id=tRYZAAAAYAAJ&pg =PP7&output=text

"Young Heiress Says She's Living Real 'Dog's Life'." *The Telegraph,* April 20, 1968.http://news.google.com/newspapers?nid=2209& dat=19680420&id=y41jAAAAIBAJ&sjid=_XkNAAAAIBAJ&pg =3717,5824511

ABOUT THE AUTHOR

Micah Hanks is a writer and researcher whose work addresses a variety of unexplained phenomena. Over the last decade, his research has taken him into studies of the more esoteric realms of the strange and unusual, as well as cultural phenomena, human history, and the prospects of our technological future as a species as influenced by science. He is author of *Magic, Mysticism and the Molecule*, and writes for a variety of magazines and other publications such as *FATE Magazine*, *UFO Magazine*, *The Journal of Anomalous Sciences*, and *New Dawn*. Hanks has also appeared on numerous TV and radio programs, including National Geographic's *Paranatural*, the History Channel's *Guts and Bolts*, CNN Radio, and The Jeff Rense Program. He also produces a weekly podcast that follows his research at his popular Website, www.gralienreport.com. Hanks lives in the heart of Appalachia near Asheville, North Carolina.